Unlocking Your Spiritual Potential

D0067896

Unlocking Your Spiritual Potential

A Twelve Step Approach

Grant R. Schnarr

Cover Design:
Scott Wannemuehler

Library of Congress Catalog Number
89-82666

ISBN 0-87029-226-9

©1990 Grant R. Schnarr
Published by Abbey Press
St. Meinrad Archabbey
St. Meinrad, IN 47577

To Cathy

Contents

Acknowledgments

Gratitude is definitely part of this spiritual program. Therefore, I begin this book by thanking those who made it possible. It could not have been written without the help of many sources. The first of these sources is the original Twelve Steps Program of Alcoholics Anonymous. These Steps have been adapted, with permission from AA World Services, Inc., for the use of those who desire to grow spiritually.

There are a variety of other sources of inspiration which I want to mention. Clearly, the Bible has been and will continue to be a great inspiration for me. I also acknowledge the works of the eighteenth-century Swedish theologian, Emanuel Swedenborg, whose ideas are included here. His works are little known today but are worthwhile reading.

Also, I thank Rev. Michael Cowley for the initial concept of this new program, Rev. Frank and Louise Rose for the idea of using tasks, and Peter Rhodes for some of the tasks themselves. Each of these people is heavily involved in their own spiritual growth programs.

I thank my wife, Cathy, and the Rev. Eric Carswell for their unending support, and Elizabeth Schnarr, and especially Susan S. King for all her work in editing the original manuscript.

Finally, I express my love and respect for the special men and women whom I have met and come to know over the years in the various Twelve Step Programs. I stand in awe of their complete honesty, courage, and desire to change their lives for the better. They have shown me through their stories that every person has a chance to become happy and spiritually rich, no matter what unfortunate circumstances he or she may have experienced.

Introduction

The underlying philosophy of the Twelve Steps has been in existence for a long time. Many different groups of people have used the Steps to overcome their compulsions or character disorders. Alcoholics, drug addicts, overeaters, individuals addicted to sex, cigarettes, or gambling, those who have emotional disorders, are codependent, or have relationship problems use these Steps. Twelve Step Programs continue to spring up all around the world to help people deal with their specific needs and to find a more healthy, happy, and spiritual life.

Why are these Steps so useful to help people overcome their compulsions? Why are they so universally helpful to those who choose to use them? Is it just a fluke that a couple of drunks banded together in order to stay sober and ended up creating some steps which give every person who chooses to incorporate them into his/her life the ability to not only become freed from his particular addiction or compulsion but also to find genuine happiness and spirituality in his life? I suggest it is more than a fluke or coincidence.

As noted above, the underlying philosophy of the Twelve Steps has been in existence for a long time. These Steps are said to have originated with the formation of Alcoholics Anonymous, but the approach of the Twelve Steps for achieving a happy, spiritual life is not unique to any self-help program. These Steps— called by other names, sometimes condensed into more or fewer steps, and sometimes not worded exactly the same—have existed in many religions, philosophies, and psychologies throughout the ages. They are based on basic principles of human psychological and spiritual development.

Because of this, these Steps work not only for the addictive-compulsive person but also for others. Anyone who desires to grow spiritually can benefit dramatically from following the Twelve Step Program. By working through these Steps regularly and thoroughly, a person will find a new sense of freedom from the destructive tendencies within: guilt, fear, anger, want, resentment, and a whole lot more, and also a completely new way of life. Those who use this Program for spiritual growth find a happiness and a peace of mind they did not know existed. They undergo a spiritual awakening. They become aware of people, themselves, their God in a new way which brings sheer joy to their lives. They come into a new relationship with their God which is not based on a blind faith and obedience but a knowing, loving, heartfelt, and free union with their Maker. They come into a life which can be called truly spiritual.

In the following chapters each of the Twelve Steps is discussed at length. I give practical advice on how to incorporate these Steps into one's life and explain why each of these Steps works and why we should follow them. At the end of each chapter, I suggest several tasks to help the reader understand and begin to implement each Step. It is my hope that this book goes much deeper than other books into the underlying philosophy of the Twelve Step Program and by this means gives the reader a greater understanding of the reason for these Steps, the way they may be used in one's life, and the benefits that result from following them. In this way those who desire may begin their personal journey of spiritual growth with some understanding of where they are going and how to get there, and will experience the comfort of knowing that they *will* get there if they are persistent.

The Twelve Steps for Spiritual Growth, adapted from the Twelve Steps for Alcoholics Anonymous, are as follows:

1. We admitted we were powerless over our destructive tendencies and that when we followed them our lives became unmanageable.
2. Came to believe that a Power greater than ourselves could bring us true sanity.
3. Made a decision to turn our will and our lives over to the care of God *as we understood Him.*
4. Made a searching and fearless moral inventory of ourselves.

5. Admitted to God, to ourselves, and to another human being the exact nature of our wrongs.
6. Became entirely ready to have God remove all these defects of character.
7. Humbly asked Him to remove our shortcomings and began a new life.
8. Made a list of all the persons we had harmed and became willing to make amends to all.
9. Began to make amends, to do good, to be honest and faithful in all our affairs, and to walk humbly with our God.
10. Continued to take personal inventory and when we were wrong promptly admitted it.
11. Sought through prayer and meditation to improve our conscious contact with God *as we understood Him,* praying only for knowledge of His will for us and the power to carry that out.
12. Having had a spiritual awakening as the result of these steps, we tried to carry this message to others and to practice these principles in all our affairs.

This Twelve Step Program works; there is no doubt about that. The spiritual life is real, fulfilling, and attainable. Turn the page and begin your journey. It is a journey with many hills and valleys, a journey with obstacles and pitfalls, but every step of the journey is a step closer to the true meaning of life and to everything the more noble part of you ever wanted to be.

The Twelve Steps of Alcoholics Anonymous

1. We admitted we were powerless over alcohol—that our lives had become unmanageable. 2. Came to believe that a Power greater than ourselves could restore us to sanity. 3. Made a decision to turn our will and our lives over to the care of God *as we understood Him.* 4. Made a searching and fearless moral inventory of ourselves. 5. Admitted to God, to ourselves, and to another human being the exact nature of our wrongs. 6. Were entirely ready to have God remove all these defects of character. 7. Humbly asked Him to remove our shortcomings. 8. Made a list of all persons we had harmed, and became willing to make amends to them all. 9. Made direct amends to such people wherever possible, except when to do so would injure them or others. 10. Continued to take personal inventory and when we were wrong, promptly admitted it. 11. Sought through prayer and meditation to improve our conscious contact with God *as we understood Him,* praying only for knowledge of His will for us and the power to carry that out. 12. Having had a spiritual awakening as the result of these steps, we tried to carry this message to alcoholics and to practice these principles in all our affairs.

(The Twelve Steps reprinted for adaptation with permission of Alcoholics Anonymous World Services, Inc.)

Step One

"We admitted we were powerless over our destructive tendencies and that when we followed them our lives became unmanageable."

If we want to experience any type of personal spiritual growth, we must first realize that we have a problem. We suffer from some destructive tendencies that cause misfortune and unhappiness in our lives and without help we are powerless over these tendencies. Some of us have no difficulty recognizing this fact; we have become familiar with our destructive tendencies and know where they lead when we follow them. People who suffer from addictions, compulsions, or emotional defects know these tendencies all too well. However, many people find the idea of powerlessness over the course of their own lives difficult to accept.

Powerless

Are we, indeed, powerless? Perhaps when we hear that suggestion, something inside us rebels against it. After all, since we were very young we were trained to go out and conquer the world, make a good life for ourselves, pursue a career, start a family, and become whatever we wanted to be. Many of us have become successful in our businesses, have married and raised families, formed friendships, and prosper in so many ways. Certainly we are quite capable of effecting changes or making things happen in our lives. Certainly we have an ability to build, change, mold, even create a life for ourselves.

However, we sometimes find ourselves powerless. Often, we set out to do something good or constructive yet it ends up all wrong. There are those times when our own sense of power and control works against us and brings an outcome we really didn't want. There are other times when we knowingly take an action that is hurtful but can't seem to help ourselves. Is there something within us over which we have very little—if any—power? Let's explore this question with a few illustrations.

John, a father in his late thirties, has been working hard to support his wife and son, spending long hours at work and taking business trips that keep him away from home many weekends of the year. He finally receives a weekend off and hopes to get reacquainted with his son with whom he hasn't spent much quality time in quite awhile. His son asks him to teach him to play baseball; he is delighted to have the chance for some quality time with his child. They eagerly grab the bat, the ball, a couple of gloves, and head out the door to reenact the World Series. But instead of creating quality time, John finds that it takes only two or three bad throws from the child, empty swings of the bat or missed catches, until his impatience takes over. He hears it in his voice and gestures as he tries to teach his son the right way. Soon, like so many times before, John's voice breaks out into words of anger: "I told you to keep your head up! Stand facing me! Don't be afraid of the ball! Stop crying! It wouldn't have hit you if you had been paying attention! What's the matter with you?"

Does this sound familiar? John has every intention of doing something good for his son, but his anger and impatience take over and destroy what was supposed to be a good and meaningful experience.

In another instance, Judy, a young and dedicated housewife, prepares a special dinner for herself and her husband one evening to celebrate their fifth anniversary. She cleans the house, cooks his favorite meal, lights the candles, brings out their favorite wine and the special china. She is excited at the prospect of surprising him with this grand feast when he walks in the door, but Judy's husband is a half-hour late. The meal overcooks, the candles burn a little too low, the wine grows stale. He walks in the door but, before he can explain, she lashes out at him with a fury: "Why didn't you call me? I prepared this special meal for us and now it's ruined! You knew it was our anniversary! How could you?" She storms off to sulk. Later, she comes out of her room to argue that he does this to her every year; he really doesn't love her. Even after he explains that the traffic was terrible because of a bad accident and that he could not call her, she refuses to back down. Deep inside Judy knows that she overreacted, but she feels all is lost now, regardless of the circumstances.

Think about that. Judy wanted to surprise her husband and have an enjoyable night together, but something inside her came up, took over, and actually snuffed out her hopes for an enjoyable time. What happened?

In another instance, Tom, a bachelor, goes on a date with a woman he truly likes and wishes to know better. He's been through a lot of bad experiences trying to find a life-partner. Although he attracts members of the opposite sex, they never seem to want to know him more deeply or have a serious relationship with him. On this particular date, Tom tries everything—the best restaurant, the most expensive meal, fabulous entertainment. But he recognizes two-thirds of the way through the evening that he is turning her off. He somehow manages to channel every topic of conversation toward himself and tries to impress her with stories of his greatness and wit. He can't seem to talk about anything else. He realizes that this happens every time he takes someone out—self-centeredness takes over and ruins everything.

What is happening to John, Judy, and Tom? Why do they exhibit behavior that will only cause them pain? They are not powerless to effect changes in their lives, but they are finding it difficult to control a certain part of their minds. In trying to accomplish something good and useful, a force within rises up and destroys the very thing they hoped to accomplish. John, Judy, and Tom find themselves temporarily powerless over their own destructive tendencies. They become powerless over themselves. Certainly, they are able to live fairly normal lives, but these destructive tendencies overcome them at times and cause them and others a great deal of pain.

Let's look with greater detail at two more specific instances where destructive tendencies begin to rule every facet of a person's life and, as a result, make life unhappy.

Perhaps you've known or even had a mother who needed to control everything. She made sure the children were completely and thoroughly clean, neat, and perfectly dressed every day for school. She worked continuously to ensure that the house was immaculate and in order at all times. Dinner had to be out of the oven and on the table at exactly six o'clock every evening. She always became upset if her husband was late or a child lagged coming home from school. If something in the house broke down or one of the family members caused a disruption in the day-to-day routine, she couldn't cope and would exert all the energy she could muster to bring things under control. Everything had to be under control. She controlled family activities, her husband's behavior, what the kids would be when they grew up. She was determined that by her power the whole family would live happily ever after.

What is wrong with this woman? She believes she has the power to create and maintain her world and she carries that whole world on her shoulders. She does not realize it, but she has turned her will and her life over to the destructive tendencies within herself. What is really controlling her world? It is her fears and her overwhelming concern for herself and her own sense of well-being. She has become so fearful of pain, rejection, and isolation that her life has become a never-ending mission to protect herself by trying to control every facet of her life. But she is trying to manage the unmanageable. No wonder her life becomes filled with dread as she runs to plug one hole after another in the imaginary dike she has built to keep pain out of her life. She has become virtually powerless over her destructive tendencies and inwardly her life has become unmanageable.

There are various kinds of controllers like this woman. The sad thing is that life can look so good on the outside but can be very disturbed, even unmanageable, on the inside. Sometimes a person can become outwardly successful and seem to have it all, but may fail miserably on the inside.

Look, for instance, at the business man (or woman) who ambitiously begins a career with the complete certainty that he is the grand master of his destiny. He feels no need or desire for a Power greater than himself. He is the power machine. He will create and build his company out of nothing and run it—his way—to absolute success. Working hard for years, he builds that company, buys his own building, and has one hundred employees working in ten different divisions.

But as the company grows, so does his burden. He's carrying that company. He's carrying that building with all its weight and each one of those employees on his back. His desire for control becomes out of control. He recognizes that he doesn't have to have his hand in every single division to make things work well.

He realizes he is run ragged trying to be at every meeting or sale. But when he takes a break from these activities, he has that terrible feeling he should be there. Moreover, if the slightest problem develops, he feels anguish because it confirms his notion that if he had been there it would not have happened. He continues to work feverishly, controlling as much as possible to ensure success. Anything he is unable to control haunts him. To the casual observer, he appears to be a perfect success, but inwardly he is failing. His life is unmanageable.

This man, like the woman, is trying to do the impossible. He believes he has the power and total responsibility for his world and he carries that world on his shoulders. His destructive tendencies are running his business, and the most powerful of all these tendencies is his fear of failure.

Even more troubling are the cases of individuals who give over their entire lives to destructive tendencies, relinquishing their will and surrendering completely to their feelings of guilt. They are consumed in efforts to make up for past mistakes, trying to heal a wound that never seems to heal. There are people, also, whose lives are dedicated to ego satisfaction. They must keep proving to themselves that they are special. They try to impress the most important person in the world, a person who never seems to be satisfied with their efforts—themselves. There are people who are constantly running—running from themselves, from reality, from responsibility, from hurt, from the possibility of rejection. Outwardly all of these people may appear to be leading fairly normal lives, but inside life is increasingly unmanageable; they don't know what happiness is. They are powerless over their own destructive tendencies and have relinquished to them all authority and control.

What do we have in common with these people? Everything! We are John, the father who loses patience with his son. We are Judy, the disgruntled housewife. We are Tom, the narcissistic young man. We are the neurotic mother and the fearful businessman trying to control the whole world. These are not particularly strange people with a strange disease. They are typical human beings like you and me. We all go through times of guilt, egotism, escapism, and low self-esteem. We all suffer from destructive tendencies at times, and the more we follow them the more they control our lives and make our lives unmanageable.

Destructive tendencies

What are these destructive tendencies? Why do they exist and where do they come from? Where they come from must be left to the decision of the individual, according to personal religious and philosophical beliefs. Every religion has its own answer to this question. Some say these destructive tendencies are built within our nature; others suggest it is the devil working through us; still others tell us that these tendencies come from chemicals in our brain or that they are the effects of our environment. Each person must choose his or her own philosophy.

When it comes to practical application, does it really matter where these destructive tendencies come from? It would help to know, but whether they are from hell or heredity, from environment or chemicals in our brain, we still have them and we still must deal with them. The point is, they exist in everyone from every race, language, or creed. Call them what you will: character defects, evils, neuroses, hang-ups. They are our fears, wants, selfishness, delusions, hatred, lusts, anger, contempt, foolishness, pride. They are real; they hurt. They are powerful and when we follow them they lead to pain, disillusionment, and, eventually, utter devastation.

The lower self

The problem with believing we are not powerless is that we then tend to believe we are all-powerful, and believing that we are all-powerful then leads to believing that we are God. Instead of looking to any other source of love or wisdom or happiness, we look for these things in ourselves. We believe we are the source of all we need. What's wrong with this belief? What's wrong is that it simply is not true. When we rely on ourselves alone as the source of our guidance and happiness, we shut the door to any higher or greater Power outside ourselves. We give the power seat over to the baser, more animalistic part within us which steers us on a course of misfortune.

These baser qualities taken together are our lower self. This lower self is the instinctive animal within us. It is very much a part of us and, surprisingly enough, we need it. It is true that this lower self contains our fears, our love for self, our desire for gratification, but these desires also have their rightful place within us. Without fears we wouldn't avoid danger, without self-love we wouldn't protect ourselves, and without a desire for gratification we wouldn't eat or mate or provide for ourselves. We need this lower self. It serves us but it should not rule us. Therein lies the problem. When we reject the notion of a Power greater than ourselves, we give the reins of authority to this lower self within us. It takes over and turns what was once constructive into something destructive. We begin to fear too much, to love self to the detriment of others, to take and take and take without thought of the outcome. This lower self becomes like an animal which keeps eating until it dies as a consequence of its insatiable appetite. Instead of serving us, it begins to rule us and to hurt us.

This lower self is bent on self-satisfaction, but when it rules it becomes a self-destructing force. When we do not rely on a higher Power to show us the path to happiness, we make this lower self our supreme authority. How we judge the good in our lives becomes judged not according to what might be best for us or others, not what might be best for us in the long run, but what feels good now: the quick fix, the false sense of security and apparent love, the cheap thrill and immediate sense of self-satisfaction.

We see this in the mother who dominates her family. She seeks a false sense of security by going for the quick fix. She forces her husband and children to act in a certain way so she can feel good; she is not concerned for their welfare. We also see this with the father who loses patience while playing ball with his child. He does not really think about the most constructive way to behave with his child; he turns his life over to that lower self which has no patience or love whatsoever. That part of him does not even want to be there. It would rather be watching television and sucking down a few beers, so the destructive tendencies come forth and the man yells and makes derogatory comments to his child.

There are many examples to show how this lower self operates in everyone's daily life. It tells us to be sneaky in business dealings, to cheat or lie, believing fully that this kind of behavior will bring success. It tells us that to hit back hard and fast is the best and most satisfying way when someone has wronged us. Our lower self believes that the grass is always greener on the other side of the fence and tries to persuade us to give up the good things we have: peace of mind, dignity, even our marriage or friends. It tells the mother to dominate her family if she wants to find happiness or the wife to shout at the husband before she learns the facts. It tells the businessman to continue to worry about his company because if he stops the whole thing will fall apart.

We might say, "Big deal! What's the great harm?" But this same lower self causes people to hurt, not only verbally but physically. It is this lower self which is responsible for all hurt and pain, for all cruelty and inhumanity. When it is not ruled by a higher Power it becomes impulsive, selfish, hateful. The lower self is not only responsible for impatience, laziness, indifference, neglect, but also for every case of child abuse, assault and battery, rape, and murder. It is responsible for all evils in the world.

Unmanageable

How unmanageable can life become for us? We can see that the more we follow this lower self and its destructive tendencies, the more outwardly unmanageable our circumstances become. Even if we never commit any crime or do anything society may call immoral, we can still suffer inwardly from an unmanageable life. We can gain the whole world by following these tendencies but lose our soul. Outwardly, we may achieve our every dream, but inside we feel empty, lost, spiritually bankrupt, and devastated. Why? Because the lower self is never happy with life as it is. If we search for happiness in these destructive tendencies, we often lose the very thing we wanted in the first place. Instead of finding happiness, we know only frustration. Instead of fulfillment, we suffer from hunger and want. Instead of peace of mind or security, we have a bag full of fears—and we're inside the bag! These baser feelings always lead to actions which take us away from our goal.

Let us return to the mother/wife who wants to control everything. She wants a good marriage and a good family. Fair enough. But how does she fulfill this desire? Since she has turned over her control to the destructive tendencies within her— her fears and self-centeredness—she tries to create the perfect family through manipulation. Through subtle and not so subtle means, she makes sure her husband acts the way she thinks a husband should act and her children are bullied into fulfilling her dreams for them. The children then find themselves acting the way Mom wants them to act when they are around her and the husband seems to be the perfect husband. But they are puppets. They act this way because of fear. Moreover, the woman herself is not happy. Outwardly she seems to have what she wants, but in her heart she knows something is missing. Furthermore, she can't control the missing part because it is inside her husband and children, in how they think and feel about her. This lack of power over their feelings drives her crazy. She feels pain. She feels unloved and inwardly rejected by her family yet she can do nothing about it. Her destructive tendencies make her worst fears come true.

Look at the motivation of the businessman who is carrying the weight of his company on his own shoulders by what he believes is his own power. His fear of failure forces him to harness the company on his back and to monitor every branch of the business. He can build the company into a highly successful corporation and virtually kill himself trying to control it, but he will never be happy. That awful fear does not know the meaning of happiness or contentment. It is a destructive inclination that is never satisfied. Without a higher Power leading him in a different direction, he is doomed to serve this fear.

We may not turn into a monster when our impatience or anger breaks out at our children or spouse, but what prevents us from remaining that impatient and angry person for the rest of our lives or even becoming worse? Nothing. In fact, we do get worse and make ourselves and everyone around us more unhappy. We can live what seem to be very normal lives on the outside, but without that higher Power guiding us away from the control of those destructive tendencies, our lives become a mess on the inside.

Hitting bottom

To achieve real happiness and spiritual life we must realize that our lives become unmanageable when we rely on ourselves alone. We have to "hit bottom." For an alcoholic, "hitting bottom" is recognizing that he or she is indeed powerless over alcohol and must get help. Some people have "higher bottoms" than others (and this has nothing to do with their physique). Some people see the writing on the wall when they miss their first day of work because of alcohol, or they almost demolish the car while under the influence. They are the lucky ones. Others have to kill someone in a car accident before they realize how out of control their lives have become.

When it comes to our spiritual lives we must also hit bottom. We must come to see the hurt we can cause ourselves and others when we follow our destructive tendencies. We, like the alcoholic or compulsive person, must see that by ourselves we are powerless over these destructive tendencies. The more we allow them to run us the more unmanageable life becomes, within and without.

But the wonderful thing is, we do not have to let these tendencies destroy us before we come to this realization. We can hit bottom with our imagination. We can see without actually doing certain destructive actions that they will hurt us or others, and what the consequences are. We do not have to hurt someone physically to know cruelty. We do not have to commit adultery to know lust, and we do not have to steal to know covetousness. Neither do we have to lie to know deceit. We can know all these things without acting them out. We can recognize our powerlessness over them without having to experience that powerlessness in some catastrophic way.

Hopefully we can hit bottom spiritually before we crash to the bottom in our natural lives—and come to see that only a Power greater than ourselves can bring true sanity and order to our lives. When we come to this recognition, we then stop running our own show and begin to allow a Power greater than ourselves to help us. We say, "OK God, or whoever you are, I lost the game when I played on my own. It's your turn now." Amazingly, when we say this from the heart, a higher Power does move into action and begins to order our life and helps us win the game.

When we admit we are powerless over our destructive tendencies we begin to glimpse another reality and, for the first time, that persuasiveness of the lower self is broken. For the first time, we begin to feel real or genuine control over our lives. For the first time we feel a warm and loving presence—our higher Power—which gives us that control, comforts us, and gives us peace.

When we finally hit bottom and come to see and admit that we need a higher Power, God, as we understand God, can begin to work within us because now we are inviting God in. We open a door and allow God to enter us, take charge, and move us in the right direction. No longer do we listen and blindly follow those destructive voices within us. We have basically confessed that they will lead us nowhere but downward. We recognize with the heart, perhaps for the first time in our lives, that we are not God; we are not all-powerful. In fact, we have no power without God, and this our destructive tendencies have proved. We are tired of their tyranny. Even when we come to this recognition, we are ready to move forward toward a true spiritual life. We leave the slavery of our own destructive tendencies and head out toward the promised land of spirituality, a land flowing with milk and honey, a land of happiness and fulfilled dreams. We are ready for true sanity, happiness, and spiritual life.

TASKS: Becoming aware of your powerlessness and your lower self

1. Reflect on the troubled areas in your life. To what degree do you have power to change these for the better? Write down those areas you recognize and have tried to change but seem powerless to do so.

2. When you become aware of a destructive emotion in yourself, notice what thoughts come with it. If you have a negative thought, observe the emotions that come with it and how quickly they arrive. When a negative emotion arises, experiment with stopping the negative thought. Notice changes in the emotions.

3. When you become aware of a negative emotion in yourself say, "It is _____from the lower self and I don't have to be_____." Notice the results.

Step Two

"Came to believe that a Power greater than ourselves could bring us true sanity."

Essentially, Step Two suggests that prior to this Step we may not have been sane. In fact, it infers that in our past we were clearly insane. For some, this is hard to believe. But Step Two also leads to some positive changes in our character. By means of a higher Power we can be brought not only to a truer sanity but also to a state of genuine happiness and spiritual life. If you are bothered by the notion that you may not have always been completely sane, I ask you to keep reading, keep an open mind, and learn. Once we clearly define the problems, we can clearly define the solutions.

Spiritual insanity

Is it true that we are not only powerless at times but also insane? Yes, we can be, but we do not have to be. Let's explore the meaning of "insanity."

A dictionary definition of the word "insanity" describes it as having a serious mental disorder or being mentally deranged. Often such individuals cannot even take care of themselves. But Step Two is not referring to this type of insanity. People who suffer from "clinical insanity" clearly suffer from a problem which is beyond their freedom and control. Step Two refers to a type of insanity that we freely bring upon ourselves.

We come closer to this type of insanity when we look at the legal definition of insanity. Generally, the word "insanity" is used in a courtroom to mean the inability to know the difference between right and wrong. If a person is mentally incompetent and, consequently, cannot know the difference between right and wrong, then that person cannot be held responsible for his or her actions. This inability to see the difference between right and wrong is closer to the definition of the insanity we are speaking of. But the legal definition and the standard dictionary definition of insanity exclude one element that separates them from the insanity spoken of in Step Two. That ingredient is freedom. Those who suffer from clinical or legal insanity aren't completely free to choose their behavior.

The insanity we are talking about here is a type of mental derangement that we freely bring upon ourselves. It is not the inability to know the difference between right and wrong, but an unwillingness to recognize that difference.

When someone does something wrong and does not know it is wrong, we generally recognize that the person cannot be held responsible for the actions. No one can justly be held accountable for doing something in complete ignorance. But what about a person who does know the difference between right and wrong, and still chooses the wrong? Worse yet, what if he knows the difference between right and wrong and chooses to forget that difference on purpose? What if he makes a mess of his life because he freely chooses to think and do things that stand in the way of the actual goals he wants to achieve? Is that insane? Yes. That is spiritual insanity.

Spiritual insanity is knowing what is right, hearing what is right, but doing the opposite. In its most pure definition, spiritual insanity is an aversion or rejection of the truth. It is freely choosing to believe and follow something false.

Without getting caught up in an argument about what exactly truth is, this book defines truth as that essential reality which leads to good. If it leads to goodness, order, happiness, and love, then it is true. Therefore, what I call truth here is what most religions call truth: the basic laws of civility, love, and morality which lead to a happy life and a better relationship with God.

Why is it insane, then, to have an aversion toward truth? If truth is that essential reality which leads to goodness and happiness, then to be averse to that is certainly insane. Simply put, if truth is reality and we are averse to reality then we are quite spiritually insane.

So often we do turn away from what we know to be true. Perhaps we have come to see that loving our neighbor really is right and does lead to a happier, more fulfilling life. We are persuaded by the reality of this idea. It makes sense and we recognize its verity. However, so often we find the lower self controlling us and those destructive tendencies nudging, pushing, and shoving us to go against what we know is true. The most compelling thoughts tell us that love toward our neighbor is a joke, that other people are our adversaries and we must fight them. Often we reject the truth that tells us to love the neighbor and instead turn to combating him. We reject what we once knew was best and allow ourselves to be led by those base inclinations.

Moreover, the more we follow those destructive tendencies, the more we make excuses for not doing what we know deep inside is right. After acting this way for a time, we end up fully believing those excuses, denials, and false ideas. We hold them up as the absolute truth. We believe that those false ideas will lead to goodness and happiness, and we become caught in a mental trap. We come into more and more states of unhappiness and unmanageable situations, but we keep telling ourselves that we are on the right track, that happiness and fulfillment are just around the corner. Thus the insanity we suffer when we follow those destructive tendencies within is a very real mental affliction. Not only do we find ourselves being averse to the truth but we also embrace what is false. In the end, what is false we call true and what is destructive or evil we call good. When we think like this, we are spiritually insane and headed toward a good deal of self-induced unhappiness and unmanageability.

Let's explore this type of spiritual insanity with some illustrations.

Alternative paths

Imagine that we are standing before a great mountain. At the top of that mountain is happiness, fulfillment, success in life, good feelings, heaven, whatever else we desire. Each of us has a map or a set of directions. For some, this map is the Bible; for others, it is other revelations; for many it is what they have learned from others or from experience. Regardless, this map shows the truth we do know about life. Most of the directions say something like: "If you look up, there is a small crevice straight ahead of you. It is narrow but you can get through. Climb straight up through it. It may seem a bit difficult, but once you get through this crevice, there are just a few more modest slopes and then you will be at the top. This is not only the best, but it is also the safest way to get to the top of the mountain." Your map or directions may vary. Some directions tell you that their way up is the only way. Also, some maps may lead you all over the mountain before you get to the top. There are, indeed, many maps, just as there are many paths which lead to the top of the mountain.

You take a look upward to scan the situation. It occurs to you that this isn't going to be a particularly pleasant or interesting climb. You look around for possible alternatives and are struck by a tempting one to your left. You glance at your map to see if it sheds any light on this particular path and are surprised to read, "If you look over to your left, there is what appears to be a path on top of a snowbank. It looks as though you could walk ten or fifteen feet up the path and be at the top of the mountain, but it is an illusion. Don't take it! If you walk out onto that snowbank, it is going to collapse and you're going to fall twenty to thirty feet and break your leg. You might even kill yourself!" (Some versions of the map say, "Thou shalt not take the left route or thou shalt surely be smitten.")

What do we so often do? Our lower self with its destructive tendencies hates following directions and, in times like these, it takes over. After all, we think we know what is better for us than some ancient book written years ago by men who claimed they had spoken with God. At least that is what our lower self believes. We look at the map. We look at the prescribed way in front of us, and we gaze at the snowbank. Whoo-wee, that snowbank looks good! So, we go trotting out onto the snowbank. Ten feet to heaven! Nine! Eight! Suddenly the snowbank collapses under our feet. We fall just about as far as we were warned we'd fall—and we break our ankle.

Is that insane? No, that's not insane. We often test things once. What's insane is that we get up on one leg and hop back up there. We look at both routes, see the snowbank path, and take it again, thinking we will be more careful this time. We fall a second time and break a leg; we crawl back up the hill and take the same route again and every time we say to ourselves, "This time it's going to work." Now, that's spiritual insanity.

As a counselor, I have met countless people who exhibit this behavior. For example, many individuals are looking for love and a sense of unity with another human being, but they keep taking an alternate path of casual sexual relations to try to get there. Instead of achieving love, they end up in a superficial relationship. They use their temporary partner to get a quick, yet not very satisfying sense of togetherness, along with a cheap thrill. They want love and togetherness, but through selfish sexual relationships they burn out the potential for these things with that particular partner. With some, sex becomes nothing more than a temporary collusion of mutual contempt.

I knew a young girl who had a lot of problems with her family, especially her relationship with her father. She wanted to love and be loved; she really needed to touch people, to be close, to feel warm and loved. It was sad because when she came into puberty she jumped into the playground of sexual experience and went on all sorts of different sexual excursions looking for love. She wanted warmth and love, but after some very bad times it didn't take her long to come to the conclusion that there is no such thing as love, that "men stink," and that life, at least at that time, had nothing of value to offer her.

Many people keep trotting out on that alternate route looking for love. Their dreams of a life partner collapse under their feet and they hit bottom again and again with each relationship. They keep falling until they convince themselves to take a different way. They have to recognize that lust and love don't mix. If they want to get to the top of the mountain, they must build an interior relationship before they can experience an exterior one. Their minds must fall in love before their bodies fall into bed. They have to take the long road of commitment and mutual support. It may not look exciting, but when they begin to walk that path, they will soon recognize that this way is better—the way that brings the warmth and love they desire. Even the physical act of sex itself becomes more delightful when accomplished by a new attitude of commitment and giving.

Hitting the wall

Let's consider another illustration for this type of insanity. Imagine we are standing in front of a large wall; happiness is on the other side of the wall. Once again, we get a set of directions which tells us how to get to the other side. We are told, "You see this little door? If you peer through to the other side it does not look too exciting; actually, it's sort of mundane. But when you go through that door things begin to change. It becomes a place of indescribable beauty. Through this door lies happiness, joy, peace, and contentment. Take it. And by the way, anything else you might see along this wall is an illusion. Don't believe it. It is a lie and a fantasy."

So we stand there, look at the wall, and see the door. It doesn't really look too exciting. Perhaps we'll take it some day, but for now we'll just stand here and wait for other alternatives. Suddenly, other alternatives do arise; other doors begin to appear on the wall. They are nothing like the plain door we've been told to take. These are magnificent! As we peer through these doors, we see all sorts of interesting things happening. Behind some, people are counting money, holding up bags of it, and calling out for us to take them. Behind others, we see servants waiting to obey our every command. Behind still others we see tantalizing sexual scenes and people beckoning us to join them. There are hundreds of other doors. All of them reveal different enticing scenes that appear to lead to the other side.

We know what we do when our lower self is in charge. Like cartoon characters, we back up about seven or eight feet and then bolt for the door of our choosing. But as soon as we reach the door, what happens? It disappears, and with a thud we hit the wall. After all, it is an illusion. Don't forget, on the other side of the wall lies happiness. The scenes which appeared to be on the other side of the wall were fantasies of happiness. Those doors don't lead to the other side, but we keep trying them, don't we? We keep backing up and running full force into those different illusions until we are bruised and bloodied. Sometimes we recognize the pain we cause ourselves and think twice before we try the same route again, but a slightly different door always seems to open up to us. We leap at it believing that this time the fantasy might be real and we just might end up on the other side.

Can you imagine walking down the street and seeing someone running into a wall over and over again? Would you think the person insane? Of course. But in our spiritual lives, we do that sort of thing all the time.

Some might argue that we don't really do these things. But consider: we're told that if we love, we will be loved. Yet what do we do? We hate. Give, they say, and it will be given back to you. Instead, we take. We don't want people to reject us, right? But often we reject them before they can reject us. We want to share warmth, love, and companionship with others. But what do we do? We build walls around ourselves so people can't get in and we won't be hurt. Often, when we let our lower self control us, we go against what we know is true and will bring true happiness.

One example of hitting the wall is in the realm of marriage and infidelity. How many married people have experienced the illusion that they will find happiness in an affair? Perhaps they have grown tired of their partner's treating them badly or ignoring them, tired of the low self-esteem they feel in their marriage relationship. Then someone comes along who shows an interest in them. The illusory door to happiness suddenly appears. If they follow their destructive feelings, they pursue the interested party and have an affair. But I've never met anyone who has made it through the wall. They hit it hard. Perhaps they hoped to find self-esteem through that door. Instead, they smack against a wall of self-degradation and pain. Many feel absolutely worthless. They do not experience happiness and bliss, only sorrow and hurt, and the extramarital relationship may destroy the marriage partner and cause the children pain for a lifetime.

People make mistakes and anyone can suffer from temporary spiritual insanity. But the more we believe in illusions the more insane our thinking becomes. The more we justify our actions and make excuses for the doors we choose or the paths we take, the deeper our insanity becomes. Moreover, the further we pursue those illusions, the more we suffer from mental and emotional affliction that the destructive tendencies within us bring.

A higher Power

There is only one real solution. After we hit the wall enough times, we must recognize that there has to be something or someone outside of ourselves which can show us a truer reality. Somewhere along the line we need to let go of our preconceived notions of what we believe will bring happiness and begin to seek a higher and more powerful Entity to lead us on a different way, a Power greater than ourselves that can bring true sanity, happiness, and spiritual life.

This higher Power waits diligently for us to call, desiring nothing more than to have us let go of our burdens, stop believing in illusions, and start believing and following him. This higher Power will lead us through the proper door, leading us every step of the way through that crevice and up the mountain. Every step in that direction gives us the sense of self-worth, contentment, happiness, and peace that we've searched for in our lives.

In the beginning, it may be difficult to believe in this higher Power. In other Twelve Step Programs, the higher Power is, initially, the group itself. This is a good start. Any higher power is better than the power of our own destructive tendencies. Many people have rejected the notion of God as that power simply because of the teachings in churches. They were taught that God is an angry God who will punish them if they do not follow certain teachings or that God is indifferent toward them and their problems. It is good that people have left these insidious visions of God behind. Perhaps we can accept the possibility that there is a God of a different nature. We can learn to believe in a God who loves us no matter what, who would never reject us but is always willing to come and fill us with a wonderful presence. We can come to believe in this Power greater than ourselves who created us for only one purpose: to have a loving relationship with him and to share that love with our neighbor. That is a God I can learn to love and trust and believe in.

At times it takes a leap of faith to recognize the reality of God. But it is not a blind leap. It is not the kind of faith where a person closes his eyes and clings to a concept of God simply because he is afraid to face the possibility of God's nonexistence. It is not faith whereby a person tries to convince himself and others that it works solely for the reason that he is afraid to admit it might not work. Rather, this good leap of faith is a leap with understanding, not one of blind acceptance or doubt, but one of accepting the possibilities with an open mind.

There are two types of doubt related to believing or not believing in God: a negative doubt and a positive doubt. Negative

20

doubt leads to spiritual folly and insanity. It believes only what the senses tell us. It says, "I'm going to believe only what I can see, hear, touch, taste, smell, and feel." When we practice this philosophy we shut the door to spirituality, denying it before we even explore it. We are saying that heaven, hell, God, and whatever we cannot grasp with our senses does not exist. Under this philosophy, what is our source of authority? Our lower, more animalistic self with its destructive tendencies tells us what is true according to what feels good. This leads, not to a satisfying way of life, but to one of frustration and discontent.

Positive doubt does not believe blindly but keeps an open mind. It says, "I don't understand it, but I'm not going to deny it. I will try to live by it to see what happens." The authority here is obvious—a higher Authority. Moreover, what happens next makes a great difference.

What happens when we have this positive attitude? On a natural level, when we choose to believe in God and his power we gradually begin to see God in things around us: the beauty of nature, expressions on the faces of others, in myriads of unusual coincidences which are not really coincidences but planned actions of an invisible but loving force. Phone calls resolving old issues, subtle warnings of dangers, unexpected money to pay unexpected bills, voices suggesting alternate courses of action which later become apparent—all these point to a higher Power directing the entire world-show. Most people who have had this kind of experience know what I am suggesting. To experience God's presence does become a bit scary at times. God appears in front of us, yet leaves us free to doubt his existence.

Do these so-called coincidences start after we believe in God? No. God has been leading us all along but we haven't noticed. Now our eyes and ears are open to see and hear.

That, however, is not the most important part of this process. What is important in our accepting this higher Power and allowing him to come into our lives is that we feel his presence within us. It is not something we just imagine. We know! We know God exists because we can feel him. We have felt this awesome power working within us to put down the destructive forces and to set us free from their bondage. The fact that our lives change in dramatic ways is testimony to God's existence. But if we had not believed, these things would never have taken place.

It works

Those who are skeptical might ask, "How do I know this will work for me? Am I really going to change if I make this leap in faith and accept a higher Power by following these Steps?" Returning to the Twelve Steps for alcoholics and addicts, we can see what these Steps have done for other skeptics. These people suffered greatly from difficulties they could not overcome until they came to believe in this higher Power and called upon him. If it works with these serious and devastating problems, why won't it work for those who may be dealing with more subtle shortcomings or day-to-day upsets?

People who came to believe in a Power greater than themselves through AA, NA, or other Twelve Step groups were not saved from just petty shortcomings or problems. Some were saved from terrible lives. They weren't saved from just desiring to take people's possessions; they stole so they could keep their habit going. They weren't saved from a few times of lust and fantasy; some were saved from living the life of whores and whoremongers. They weren't saved from a lack of self-esteem in their lives; they were saved from utter self-hatred and from waking each morning with the strong desire to kill themselves.

Taking the Second Step really works. Believing in a Power greater than themselves, this Power saved them from the sheer hell they had been experiencing. If it can save these, then it can save anyone. But one must have enough trust in God to be able to say, "I don't understand it completely, but I'm going to try to live by God's teachings." When we do that, our lower self with its destructive inclinations is no longer our authority and guide. The Source of power, love, and happiness becomes our authority and our guide. We no longer need to turn aside to fantasy and illusion in our search for happiness. We turn to the truth and that truth makes us free.

When we finally take the right path or walk through the right door, things begin to happen. We realize what sanity really means. Our base feelings no longer rule us and drive us to acts of insanity, anguish, and despair. The higher Power within begins to guide us through our own reasoning. We become rational beings capable of making rational choices that lead to goodness, happiness, and peace. That story begins with the next Step.

TASKS: Separating fact from fiction; recognizing a higher Power

1. Observe your lower self lying:
   a. saying to yourself and others what is not true
   b. rationalizing, making excuses by lying to yourself
   c. exaggerating externally or internally
   d. talking with authority about something you know little or nothing about; for example, the federal budget
2. Stop the lying, as soon as you become aware of it.
3. Force yourself to talk to God at least once each day and notice what effect this has on your perception of his presence.

Step Three

"Made a decision to turn our will and our lives over to the care of God as we understood Him."

Let Go Let God

By the time we are ready to take Step Three we have come to realize how powerless we are over our destructive tendencies and how insane our actions can be. Now it's time to do something with these realizations. We gradually begin to hand over control of our lives to that Power greater than ourselves. We begin to "let go and let God."

A parable of letting go

An effective illustration for this step is a story from the New Testament. The New Testament is rich with specific symbolism which deals directly with spiritual and psychological development. This is especially true of the story of Jesus walking on the water (Mt 14:22-33). This story is for anyone because of its obvious lessons about turning our will and life over to God's care. Think about God as you understand God, but don't reject the story. One can learn so much from it.

Immediately after Jesus performed the miracle of feeding five thousand people with five loaves and two fish, he told his disciples to get into a boat and go to the other side of the Sea of Galilee while he prayed on the mountaintop. It was late and darkness was beginning to fall, but they did as Jesus told them, boarding the boat and heading off across the sea to reach the far shore.

While they were out, a storm arose. The wind began to roar, and the waves battered the boat so much that they could not reach land. They rowed for a long time, fighting the wind and the waves. They rowed all night in a futile attempt to reach the other side, a mere five miles away. But the wind increased and the waves nearly capsized the boat.

The disciples were afraid and while they struggled to keep the boat afloat, they suddenly saw someone walking on the water toward them. Thinking it was a ghost, they cried out in terror.

But it was Jesus and he calmly called to them, "Be of good cheer. It is I. Do not be afraid." Then Peter, who always seemed to be the spokesman for the disciples, said, "Lord, if it is you, command me to come to you on the water." Jesus said, "Come." Peter stepped out of the boat and began to walk on the water. But his attention drifted as he felt the wind and saw the water whipping around him. He began to doubt. Becoming afraid, he started to sink. "Lord, save me!" he called, and immediately Jesus grabbed him and held him up. He was rescued.

As they boarded the boat, the winds ceased and a calm descended over the sea. Imagine, too, the rays of the morning sun beginning to show forth on the horizon. The disciples in that boat knelt before him in awe.

This is a beautiful and dramatic story. We see Peter's genuine faith and his willingness to let go of the boat and put his trust in Jesus. Symbolically, this story touches each of our lives. Jesus, Peter, the boat, the wind and the waves all symbolize a part of us and our spiritual development.

Taking the journey alone

We are all on a journey to serve a purpose, to fulfill a mission, and to find happiness, contentment, and life's meaning. It is God as we understand God who sends us on this journey, encouraging us to seek these things, promising that he will join us on the other side. Thus, from birth until death we are on a voyage to find these things.

Each of us has a boat that carries us on this voyage of life. Our boat holds us up. It represents our beliefs and our preconceived notions of what life is all about. Our beliefs, chosen from experience, from others, from religion, carry us on the voyage. Each of these beliefs is a section of that boat and forms the vessel. In the comfort of these beliefs we set off on our voyage.

But what often happens? We embark on that journey heedless of who sent us and why. We leave God or a higher Power behind, believing we can find happiness and contentment without him. As we move into life without him, though, it isn't long before life appears to be working against us. We attempt to change

tter by our own power, but we get nowhere.
es whip up within us like a contrary wind
us in every direction. They prevent us
toward the goal and the happiness we

ssful attempts at rowing all night to
olize our own powerlessness and de-
y work to change our lives—to be
more content—but without that
Like the disciples, we row and row

rustrating sense of impotence. Consider
pects you might want to change in your life,
rity or lack of self-esteem. Most of us suffer from
the time or another. Those who suffer from insecurity
know how difficult it is to do anything about it. Perhaps we've
tried to overcome it by promising ourselves repeatedly that we
are going to stop feeling that way, but nothing happens. We may
read self-help books or use various techniques to gain a sense of
self-worth. Maybe we use affirmations or practice positive thinking techniques to help us feel better about ourselves. Occasionally we may make a little headway until a situation arises—a negative comment from a spouse, a friend, or someone at work—that
triggers the sense of insecurity and worthlessness. We are swept
back to the place we were before we started working on the problem. We've gotten nowhere.

Perhaps insecurity is not a problem for you. Instead, you may
find yourself filled with a sense of superiority over other people.
How do you overcome this air of superiority? Can you say to
yourself one day, "Gee, I'm going to stop feeling superior over
others today"? If you are really in control, why doesn't this
work? You can exert great effort to overcome this dilemma, but
where do you start? You can't beat it on your own.

How many of us are perfectionists? We can be critical of others and try to show them the "right" way to do a job. But often
enough, we are more dissatisfied with ourselves. We can't do a
good enough job even when everyone else is satisfied. Nevertheless, we continue to chide ourselves.

Destructive tendencies, therefore, prevent our moving forward
toward happiness. We row until we're exhausted from trying to

make ourselves happy. Still, we cannot do it on our own.

These tendencies not only hold us back, but they also try to sink us. From time to time they cause great storms in our lives and toss us about unmercifully. We cling to our boat—what we thought was right—tired, frightened, and confused.

For example, twinges of insecurity are inevitable, but a person's insecurity can go beyond a small distraction and turn into self-hatred. We can become angry with ourselves for not being stronger or up to par. Something inside rises up to hurt us. New feelings of self-degradation and even self-destruction assault us. We recognize we shouldn't feel this way but we seem unable to help ourselves. These destructive tendencies whip about in our minds and cause great distress. They push us around, control us, and try to bring us down.

A subtle sense of superiority over other people may not seem to be a problem, but a terrible fear of failure can accompany it. If we believe we are so great and put on a front not only before others but also within ourselves, then a quiet inner voice begins to nag: "Well, if you're so great, you better not fail." People who suffer from this sense of superiority may also suffer from a terrible fear of failure. They work to do their best in everything they do because they are afraid if they don't their lives might fall apart. If they don't keep rowing their boat, they fear they will sink.

The presence within

During these spiritual storms, we feel alone and in the dark. But we are not alone. That higher Power has not abandoned us, but comes to us just as Jesus came to his disciples. Have you ever had that feeling? Perhaps you have gotten into a jam and feel you have failed completely. That is the time when the higher Power, the Presence within us, appears at a distance. He doesn't push or force himself on us, nor does he call. He simply appears on the horizon of our minds waiting for us to recognize and invite him into our consciousness.

What is this appearance of the Presence within? It can be just a sensation that frees us from feeling distraught or alone and abandoned. This Presence within may be sensed as a distant promise of inner peace if only we can let go. Often this Presence appears in the form of our own conscience, quietly, unobtrusively showing us another way to go in life so we don't have to rely on our own power to get to the other side.

Why is it that the disciples were afraid of Jesus when they saw him if he represents the Presence who has come to help us? The reason is that we fear we may have to change if this Presence enters our lives. We become afraid lest we lose our own will. Often we want the peace, contentment, and joy that this Presence can bring, but we don't want to change our old ways. We want the benefits but we don't want to make the sacrifice. God's teachings can appear cold and lifeless and a threat that may kill our inner life or deaden our sense of pleasure.

For example, if someone verbally slaps us on the cheek, saying something derogatory, we are ready to take immediate action to retaliate. But then we hear the words, "Turn the other cheek." These words may frighten us and we rebel inwardly. "Turn the other cheek? This person will run all over me if I turn the other cheek. I can't do that; I'll lose my dignity if I follow that teaching."

Imagine a woman who experienced abusive treatment from her parents as she grew up. She eventually leaves home, but with a great deal of resentment toward her parents. Then she remembers the phrase, "Forgive and you will be forgiven." That teaching seems frightening as she asks herself, "How can I forgive them? I don't want to be hurt again." These teachings are so frightening that they appear to harm her, not help her. She has trouble seeing their true nature, their inward healing power.

What did Jesus say to his disciples? "Be of good cheer. It is I. Do not be afraid." Goodness emerges from these teachings. We don't turn the other cheek and forgive others just because God indiscriminately chose that way for his own pleasure. It's not a practical joke. Those teachings lead to happiness, to the way to find our God and recognize him.

In the midst of these spiritual storms, we have the opportunity to turn our will and our lives over to the care of God as we understand him, but many of us don't understand him very well. Our concept of God may be very different from what or who God is. We have to accept that and be willing to let go of our old ideas.

We may have been brought up believing in a condemning

God, a God who is the playground bully who will zap us if we don't play his game. We may be afraid to view God as a loving, caring God for fear we may be wrong and the condemning God will make us pay for our mistaken ideas. But remember, Jesus spoke to his disciples saying, "Be of good cheer. It is I. Do not be afraid." We have to risk, to change our view of God to something more realistic and more helpful.

This concept of God may be more difficult for those who have tossed out the idea of a personal God and who view God as merely life itself, nature, or perhaps just the power of people. This view of God tends to picture him as an "it," as one having a heartless, machine-like quality that negates the building of a genuine relationship. Can you love an "it"? Can you build a relationship with an "it"? You may have to throw out that idea and conclude that God is, indeed, a real force in nature and in human beings, and has an identity and life of his own, with a definite personality.

It is essential to keep the mind open when God presents himself to us. In stormy times, we need to remember that we may be afraid of what we see, but we have to let go of our old concepts of God and see him as he presents himself to us now. When that Presence comes into your life in times of turmoil, it may not be the God you once learned about. Nonetheless, God is still saying, "It is I," that essence of love, that source of goodness, that beautiful being which always meant so much to you. It is your concept of God that you have deep within. It is your God coming to you.

Letting go

When spiritual storms come, we cling to our boat and peer out at this new Presence with fear and apprehension, but something inside us recognizes this Presence and is willing to let go and follow it. We may not always pay attention to this something, yet it is there. Within us is a willingness to take the risk, to let go of our preconceived notions, step out of the boat, face the storm, and seek that higher Power.

That "something" is our faith, and Peter represents it. He symbolizes our faith, our trust, our hope in that higher Power. The faith within us helps us to recall those times when the Presence

helped us. We remember times of peace when we follo
conscience rather than our destructive tendencies and were w.
ing to let go and let the Presence take charge.

Peter said, "Lord, if it is you, command me to come to you on
the water." We can envision Peter stepping out of the boat, then
walking toward Jesus. This symbolizes our personal letting go,
leaving our old ideas behind to seek that Presence in our lives.
We believe in the power of the Presence within and begin to face
the storm, to walk to him on the surface of the turbulent sea. A
miracle!

What does walking symbolize in this and other biblical stories? To walk means to live, and this is evidenced throughout the
Bible. In Psalm One we hear "Blessed is the man who walks not
in the counsel of the ungodly." This doesn't mean we should
walk through a board meeting of the national organization of
atheists. Rather, it means to live a godly life—to follow after
God and his ways.

It is important to recognize that getting out of the boat and
turning our will over to God does not imply that we turn everything over to God. God doesn't manipulate us like puppets. Peter
still had to walk; he was in charge of his actions, but the power
of Jesus kept him afloat in the storm. So it is with us. We make
the choices, take the actions, and live life to its fullest, but always rely on a new power to sustain and guide us.

Now, for the first time in our lives, we begin to perceive spiritual progress. Emotional waves seem less likely to submerge us
and the violent wind doesn't tear us apart. The presence of this
higher Power puts us in control of our lives, and we rise above
any storm. A miracle seems to take place within us.

We notice this when we meet others who have used the
Twelve Steps to recover from alcoholism or drug addiction.
These people tried everything to escape from the storms of their
addiction. Not until they let go of their old beliefs and allowed
that Presence to guide their lives were they able to live a new life
without alcohol or drugs. The addiction was gone—perhaps for
the first time in ten or twenty years—and along with it the
storms. They feel a miracle has taken place; they feel they are
walking on water, doing the impossible. This is the first spiritual
experience many alcoholics and drug addicts talk about in the
Twelve Step Program—the realization of a miracle in their lives.

Everyone can experience this kind of miracle. Suddenly, we are free of the myriad problems we once faced—problems with emotions, with sexual desires, with fears and shortcomings. We seem able to control the problems, led by a Power greater than ourselves. We are living a miracle!

We must, however, be realistic. Those feelings of elation at the beginning of a new life don't last forever, and we may lose sight of our goals. We begin to doubt. Peter didn't walk over the water, hug Jesus, and get back into the boat to live happily ever after. Life doesn't work that way. As he walked toward Jesus, Peter began to lose sight of him and began focusing more attention on the whistling of the wind and the whipping of the waves. He was afraid and began to doubt that he could walk on the water. With that doubt he started to sink.

This is symbolic in our own lives. The wind represents the negative thoughts and false ideas which whip around in our minds and howl in our ears during stormy times. Again, we see this throughout the Bible. Jesus says that those who build their house upon the rock will not be hurt by the wind, the rain, or the flood. This is symbolic of those who build their lives on a solid foundation of truth. They will not be hurt by the onslaught of these thoughts during spiritual storms. In contrast, the ungodly are purported to be like chaff which the wind drives away; they experience no higher Power and are driven by the wind—their negative thoughts.

In this particular story, the wind which concerns Peter also denotes negative thoughts. Like Peter, when we initially put our trust in this higher Power, we feel we're above the storm. We easily succeed with the help of this new Power, and the inner change delights us. But it isn't long before old thought patterns reassert themselves and negative thoughts creep in. These thoughts emerge and insinuate such ideas as "What do you mean you're over your sense of insecurity? Come on, be realistic. You are one of the lowest life forms on this earth," or "What do you mean you've stopped feeling all that resentment? You've let go of that, huh? Look around; you're being kicked all over the place. People are laughing at you. They're using you. If there's anybody who deserves to feel resentment, it's you." That's the howling wind.

These negative voices whip up emotions, filling us with false ideas that cause fear and doubt. They say, "What is all this about changing your life and being on top of things? You can't change. That's the reality of the situation. Human inadequacy is all there is. There are no such things as miracles. No one can walk on water." It is all too easy to listen to these false ideas and begin to sink back into the way we once were: into selfishness, anger, resentment, depression, guilt, pain, powerlessness, and unmanageability.

What did Peter do? He was sinking, but he didn't disappear under the murky water or fall in up to his neck and then swim back to the boat a beaten man. (Sometimes we do that, though. It is a genuine relapse into old ways.) Peter remembered who was holding him up and, like a little child, he looked to Jesus and cried, "Lord, save me." And immediately Jesus took him up.

This represents the ultimate letting go and letting God. There comes the point in our spiritual development when each of us recognizes that we cannot do it ourselves. There comes a point when we realize how powerless we really are over the wind, our negative thoughts; the waves, our emotions; and the storm, our destructive tendencies. We begin to sink into our old way of life and so we cry out to the higher Power to save us.

When, in our spiritual turmoil, we call out to the higher Power, he is there to help us. He catches us and lifts us into his arms. This Presence holds and protects us like a father holding a child, protecting that child from harm. We feel the awesome power in the touch of this Presence and recognize that this is the power of Love. It is real and it can, indeed, save us from any wind, wave, or storm. This is the ultimate turning of our will and our life over to the care of God as we understand him. This is the ultimate letting go and letting God.

Then Jesus takes Peter and, together, they get back into the boat. Indeed, we go back to what we believed was right, but this time there is a difference. This time, the Presence comes with us and is at the center of our beliefs, at the center of our very being. Moreover, when this happens, a great change occurs. The winds cease and the sea becomes still. The storm is over. Serenity takes its place.

Then we know that the disciples came and bowed before Jesus, recognizing his awesome power. So too, when we experience this event in our lives, everything within us recognizes that not only does this inner Presence exist, but it also has all power, and this Presence uses that power for only one purpose: to make us happy by putting our lives in his care.

We can imagine the sun coming up over the horizon; its rays of light glisten on the calm waves and a gentle breeze from a different origin begins to stir and carries with it the message of a new day. It won't be long until we reach the other side.

TASKS: Letting go and letting God

1. This week create a task for yourself that relates to handing your life over to the care of God. It might take the form of beginning each day with a prayer such as "God, I give my life to you this day." It could take the form of pausing from time to time to ask: "God, what is your will for me at this moment?" Find a task that applies to the situation of your life at this time.

2. When a stressful situation arises and you feel out of control, ask God to take care of the problem for you: "God, this is now your problem, not mine. But I'll do my best to help you with it."

Step Four

"Made a searching and fearless moral inventory of ourselves."

The first three steps of the Twelve Step Program fit together as one unit. They help us to recognize the need for a higher Power and then encourage us to turn our lives over to the care of this Power. These beginning steps are critical for spiritual growth. They mark a turning point toward a better way of life. However, they are not enough in themselves; they are not enough to make deep and lasting changes within us which will bring genuine happiness and spirituality. We need to take Step Four: a personal inventory.

Why take an inventory?

In working the first steps, we confessed we had a need, but did we understand what that need really was? In our search for happiness and spirituality, do we understand why we are not happy? We have a general idea but no clear picture of what is really going on inside us. In the third Step we turn our will and our life over to the care of God, but we still don't know just what it is that God will do for us. We know only in a general way that we need this higher Power who will make our life better. Now in Step Four, we take an inventory of ourselves; that is, we examine ourselves to see what our needs are and how the higher Power can help.

Some may tell you that a moral inventory is not necessary to attain the spiritual life. They say that if you want to leave your problems behind and find happiness and spirituality, you must take certain actions or believe certain tenets of faith. But is this realistic? If we merely do or believe certain things without really dealing with inner motives, aren't we avoiding the problem? If our life is faulty as a direct result of our inner loves and motives, changing our actions alone or even our beliefs won't produce a better life. To achieve spirituality, it makes sense that we fix up our inner self, loves, and motives first, then go forward in life with a new heart to do good things for other people. Isn't that what Jesus meant when he said, "Cleanse first the inside of the cup and platter"?

As an illustration, what does a company do if its product starts coming out faulty from the production line? Increase productivity and create more of these faulty products? No, that wouldn't help. In the same way, if we display some faulty behavior, should we increase productivity? Should we simply do more good deeds? Of course not. The product is still faulty because something is wrong with the production line. The only way to fix it is to examine it to see where the problem lies. Likewise, we should look inside ourselves, determine why we feel bad about life, why things go sour, and then work at fixing the problem. Don't cover it over or run away from it.

Without self-examination, we never really recognize the full implications of the destructive forces which motivate us. We may never see the real harm we cause ourselves and others. Eventually, we cease to recognize the difference between the positive and the negative, the destructive and the nondestructive, the good and the evil.

We can see this in people who delight in gossiping or telling stories that reflect poorly on others so that they themselves can perhaps feel a sense of superiority. If they never reflect on what they are doing and what the underlying motivation behind their actions is, they cannot see anything wrong in their behavior or the harm that comes from it. They'll go on gossiping day in and day out, and justify what they are doing. After awhile they convince themselves they are doing a service. They say, consciously or unconsciously, "I'm telling the truth," or "I'm putting people in their proper light for others to see," or "Somebody has got to make these judgments." They become blinded to their true motivation which is less than noble.

Another example occurs in business. Among some circles it is acceptable for a married man to go on a business trip or to a convention and perhaps take a prostitute once or twice while he is away from home. If he's asked whether this isn't damaging to his marriage, he might reply, "This really doesn't have anything to do with my marriage. What's the harm as long as my wife doesn't know?" Yet, if he examines his motives and the effects of that action on his marriage and family, he will see its impact. The cold indifference a man begins to feel toward his wife and the cruelty that emerges from time to time are direct effects of his infidelity. But without some serious reflection, without something of a moral inventory, the destructive tendencies within can go unrecognized. The man sees no relationship between these tendencies and the problems which arise in his marriage.

That's a dramatic example. But the same need for self-examination applies to all of us. Have you ever done something you considered relatively harmless, not hurting anyone or getting in anyone's way. Then you discover that someone is really upset with your behavior. You might be taken aback and wonder why the other person feels that way. You didn't intend any harm, but after some personal reflection you realize there were some negative aspects about your action. And behold! There were even some negative motivations behind your actions. It's a shocker and can be disconcerting to realize that you don't always know how your actions are affecting others or what is motivating you.

As an illustration, imagine yourself in a business where you can move ahead. You are in charge of assigning jobs each week to your peers. You try to be fair and give each one the work that best suits his or her abilities. One day one of those peers comes to you and asks you bluntly why he always gets the worst jobs, the jobs that have the greatest potential for failure. He suspects you are trying to keep him from moving up. You reflect for a split second and say, "Joe, I give you those jobs because you are obviously the most competent worker I have. There's no malice in my actions." After he leaves, you think about it for a time. You realize that Joe is quite competent, probably even more competent than you. In fact, last week when you gave him that impossible job you were half-consciously considering how much less stressful life would be if he failed, knowing your job would be more secure. The more you think about it, the more you recognize that you have been holding him back from success and that the motives behind your actions were less than pure. Before this reflection you thought you were a fair person.

Another example of not recognizing motives can be found in flirtation. You and your spouse meet a new couple who are a treat to go out with. You are overjoyed at the way you personally hit it off with this couple, especially the other's spouse. You have long talks with the other's partner; you laugh, joke around, even go off together to talk about common interests that your spouses don't seem to share with you. It's innocent, you think, until your spouse confronts you with some hard questions: "Do you really think it's right for you two to go off alone? You didn't say one word to me tonight! In fact, you were too busy flirting to even look at me!" Immediately you are taken aback. "What are you talking about?" you ask. "It was perfectly innocent. Gee, you're insecure, aren't you?" But later that night or the next morning you begin to reflect on your actions. In fact, that morning when the other spouse calls and asks if you want to have lunch together and continue your talk, you recognize you have crossed that invisible line from innocent interaction into high risk. The more you think about it the more you recognize you had not only gone a little too far but also had enjoyed it a little too much. Your spouse had every reason to be upset, but it would probably not be wise to admit it.

These are simple examples of ways we can, at times, be oblivious of the motives which underlie our actions. Both of these situations exemplify some fairly common and not too harmful destructive tendencies. They can, however, become very harmful unless we recognize them and are on guard for them. A personal inventory can reveal many negative motives that might otherwise go unnoticed. Self-examination—a personal inventory—is a real eye-opener.

Step Four helps us see these underlying harmful negative motives. It helps to bring about a change for the better in areas we would not have recognized without that inventory. As an example, let's picture our lives as a beautiful verdant garden with many flowers, fruits, and vegetables. Occasionally a thorn or a weed or a thistle emerges in the garden, representative of our selfishness, our greed, our anger, our impatience. The "garden" looks ugly. We may recognize these unwanted weeds and just lop off the top to get rid of the problem—temporarily. Or we may ignore them and hope they will go away. We don't really deal with the root of the problem.

We may be enjoying the beauty of a particular flower only to notice that it is wilting; it soon dies. Something good we had been doing mysteriously goes bad. Perhaps an important relationship begins to suffer and die for no apparent reason. Something under the surface is killing the things we love. We need to look beneath the surface to determine the cause.

This is our inventory. We walk into the garden, gently push aside the flowers, and look underneath to discover the thorns and the thistles which have been choking them and certain fruits and vegetables. With this inventory, we delve below the surface to discover the destructive tendencies eating away at our lives, to admit that besides vegetables and flowers this garden has weeds, and we pray to God for the power to work at weeding the garden.

It is important that we go below the surface when we do our moral inventory. If we want to grow spiritually, it is not enough to work on improving only our outward lives. We must look within. What makes us tick? What motivates certain actions? If we deal only with the actions and ignore the motivation behind the actions, we are camouflaging the problem.

The alcoholic who has stopped drinking but has gotten no help with the fundamental problems that contributed to his drinking is a clear example of this. Recovering alcoholics who are in a Twelve Step Program call this individual a "dry drunk." He may have changed his actions, but he's still the same person on the inside and looks for the shortcut or the quick fix. He's still impatient, full of anger, and continues to suffer from guilt and depression. He still wallows in his sense of self-importance and exaltation. Yes, he's still a mess even though he has changed his actions—he no longer drinks. The alcoholic has never dealt with the real person within; he is the same drunk. That is why a Twelve Step Program is so important for recovering alcoholics. It encourages them to delve below the surface to discover their deep-seated problems. They must learn to think differently. They must learn a new way of living, not only on the exterior but also within. Only then will they truly find a new way of life, a life of sobriety, a life of peace, serenity, and fulfillment apart from alcohol.

If we really want to change, we must examine our inner self. We must alter not only our actions but also our loves, our motives, our feelings. These are all a part of us. We may refrain from doing the wrong or immoral things we love only because others will think ill of us. Sometimes we avoid a particular wrong or immoral action for fear of the law. But curbing such destructive actions alone will not change us. Although we do no physical harm to someone, the hatred and revenge may seethe within. We may refrain from immoral sexual practices but immoral sexual thoughts still plague us hour after hour. We may no longer act on these destructive tendencies, but until we come to grips with them interiorly as well as exteriorly they remain a strong inner force, causing us much unhappiness and remaining unmanageable.

How to take an inventory

There are many ways to take a personal moral inventory. Helpful guides are available from different Twelve Step groups. The method for taking the fourth Step is your own choice, but there are guidelines. A moral inventory takes time. Reserve several hours for the initial inventory to settle your thoughts and to do some quiet reflection. This won't be completed in one day. Most guides suggest that after completing an inventory, you put it away for a while and return to it later; you may want to make additions.

The inventory should be a written one since there is a great difference between superficially counting off one's shortcomings or deeds and writing them down for later reflection. Writing them gives a more objective view.

What should you write about yourself? There are many different approaches. You might want to start with a brief life history. Some people begin with childhood, writing about their reactions to events in their life. They might write, "Senior year in high school: suspended for dismantling teacher's car; Feelings: arrogance, embarrassment, resentment." Perhaps you will list five or six other significant events for that year.

The next heading could be, "College: First year," followed by a list of noteworthy deeds and the accompanying feelings. This inventory could embrace all of the college years, first job, marriage, a year-by-year recounting of your life.

Some people write two lists: their positive character traits and their negative ones. Others use the familiar "seven deadly sins"—pride, greed, lust, anger, gluttony, envy, and laziness—as a base to work from. Whether you believe in the traditional con-

Stop being the

cept of sin or not, these are some of the more universal destructive tendencies or character defects. Still others picture their feelings as different products on the shelf at the grocery. They decide which "products" are getting too much space, which shouldn't be on the shelf at all, are neglected, underpriced, or sold out. The idea should be clear. Any of these techniques can serve the purpose when you do a moral inventory.

How do you discover your inner motives? There are several ways. Besides discovering and writing what you have done, begin paying attention to your trend of thought when you are alone. Are your thoughts unselfish and constructive or selfish and destructive? Be honest and ask yourself, "What would I do if there were no laws nor anyone to look down on me?"

Perhaps life would be no different for you under these circumstances. On the other hand, maybe you sense that some destructive tendencies would readily seek expression if there were no outward restraints. If you could rob a bank and know for certain you wouldn't be caught, would you do it? Ask yourself, "What do I see as allowable? Does it match up with what other people believe is allowable? Does it match up with the teachings of most religions? If not, why not? Am I fooling myself?" When you ask these questions, you begin to see beyond the superficial self into deeper motivations, the bad ones and the good ones.

Don't look at just the negatives when you take your moral inventory; that will depress you and make you want to give up in the attempt to deal with your destructive tendencies. Get a balanced picture of yourself; recognize the positive as well as the negative. The only reason we look for these destructive tendencies is to deal with them and make our lives better.

For practical reasons, the focus is more on the negative than on the positive, but don't lose sight of the positive. A gardener who is weeding a garden will not forget that there are other things in the garden besides noxious weeds. The short-term focus may be on the weeds, but after the weeds are rooted out the garden thrives, displaying beautiful flowers and lush fruit and vegetables. That is the desired outcome.

When I attended a religious high school outside Philadelphia, a minister there brought this concept home to me. He was my religion teacher and a recovering alcoholic who knew how to talk to the students on their level. I remember distinctly his bringing home this point about getting a balanced picture of yourself. He said, "When you do this self-examination, look for the good points and the bad points to get a balance. Write these things down." I remember trying to trick the man—which high school kids are wont to do—by asking, "Sir, what if you don't have any good in you? What should you do then?"

He smiled and in a harsh, somewhat sarcastic voice said, "Schnarr, did you ever kick your grandmother down the stairs?"

"No," I replied.

"Then write that down!" he exclaimed.

There is a point to that simple, somewhat sarcastic answer. Sometimes we get into mindsets where we see just the bad; we find it difficult to see the good we do. If you have to, write down the things you haven't done. It is important. It doesn't hurt to re-mind ourselves of our own good, especially when we're feeling depressed or guilt-ridden over our condition. I might say to my-self, "Yes, I have a problem with my temper, but I've never hurt anyone. I argue a lot, but I try to be fair and am generally a for-giving person. I don't hold grudges." We might list our good qualities next to the shortcomings then say to ourselves, "Yes, I am bullheaded; I argue; I look for the quick fix in life; I am an egotist; I have a short temper. But I am also optimistic, pretty fair, basically honest, and industrious." This provides a balanced picture and helps us to maintain a sense of hope as we recognize the shortcomings that do exist in our lives.

This inventory is intended to be not only searching but also fearless. Why fearless? Because we have turned our will and our lives over to the care of God before taking this Step. This moral inventory is not the first Step. It is not the first Step because we need that higher Power when we take it; that makes it a fearless inventory.

We have already called on the higher Power to help us. We have called on God to give us the strength to overcome these de-structive tendencies. Now we are in his care when we begin to take a hard look at ourselves. He will supply us with courage and hope as we take this inventory and discover those destructive tendencies within. They may be frightening and we will discover things about ourselves that won't be fun. But the Presence within will comfort and encourage us. He tells us destructive tendencies do not have to motivate us. He tells us that we can change—with his help. We will receive new inclinations and loves for good and useful purposes. Along with these, order, peace, and joy will come into our lives. It is important to have that higher Power with us when we make this change.

One minister I know has an illustration he uses in teaching children and young people. He draws a picture of a tiny person next to a huge monster. He tells the children, "If you're all alone and are looking at those frightening things within you, you feel like a midget looking up at this looming monster." Then he adds an even larger figure of God behind the tiny person, saying, "But when you recognize that God is with you, you may still feel very small, but you're holding the hand of a big and powerful person who far overshadows this monster. You immediately realize this monster does not have any power over you at all." When our higher Power accompanies us during this inventory, we can face anything. We realize that in the presence of this higher Power these destructive tendencies have no power whatsoever over us.

After writing a list of the bad and the good within us, we need to take time to look over the list to be sure we have covered the entire gamut of our inward lives. We ask ourselves whether we've been honest in our appraisal. We must be ruthless in the search to discover ourselves and hold nothing back. If some areas of our lives are left untouched or undocumented, those problems will not just go away. Brutal honesty spares us much pain down the road by dealing with the inner problems now. Keep in mind that the higher Power is with us to protect us from harm and to comfort us during this stressful time of soul-searching.

After we take a personal inventory, we might be surprised at how we feel. We may expect to feel gloomy, depressed, and a bit guilty. That can be true. But most often we feel a sense of relief. We have taken blinders from our eyes and see ourselves clearly for the first time. Understandably, we see things about ourselves that are uncomfortable. But reflection on the Steps we've already taken reveals that we are making progress. We know that the higher Power can remove even persistent shortcomings.

After the fourth Step, we are not only relieved but we also experience another new sensation sweeping over us: a feeling of awe as we sense reality. We lose those grand illusions of ourselves. They vanish with this step. Those who suffer from egotism finally feel what life is like without a stuffy, swelled head. They can breathe for a change; it feels good to be humble. Those who suffer from overwhelming guilt realize they are not so bad after all. They are wrapped in a sense of peace—a pervasive peace within themselves—as they come to accept themselves. It is an awe-inspiring moment to feel neither pride nor guilt, to have no grand illusions, to know the truth about self—and this for the first time.

TASK: Warming up for a fearless inventory

Find one-half hour this week to sit quietly and list five emotions, behaviors, or recurring thoughts which you believe are liabilities to your spiritual growth. Then list another five emotions, behaviors, or recurring thoughts that you consider assets to your spiritual growth. In doing this project, notice any new insights or discoveries.

Step Five

"Admitted to God, to ourselves, and to another human being the exact nature of our wrongs."

Step Four and Step Five go hand in hand. After discovering the nature of one's wrongs, it is critical to admit them to God, self, and another human being. It is critical for two reasons which may seem contradictory.

First, we should confess these shortcomings so we can accept responsibility for them. Second, by accepting responsibility for these shortcomings, we can let them go and begin to break free of their grip and the burdens they place upon us.

Without this step it would be easy to take a glossary look at our shortcomings and then move on with life, never really accepting them as our own, never really dealing with them in a constructive way. Perhaps you've had someone point out one of your shortcomings. Have you listened to the criticism, taken note of it, even thought about it for a while, then found that as time passed the criticism slipped away and you continued on as before? That's my experience.

My wife, Cathy, told me that I spend too much time at work and tend to put family matters in the last place of importance. I heard that criticism, thought about it, even acknowledged its validity, but as days passed I would get caught up in occupational matters again, completely forgetting the problem. I'd continue to behave in my customary way until she'd bring the problem to my attention once again. Nothing changed until I finally got serious and took time to reflect not only on my behavior but also to admit that "Yes, I tend to put work before family." Admitting this made a big difference. I realized I had heard the problem and unconsciously, perhaps, toyed with the idea, but I didn't take responsibility for it. Admitting it to myself made it easier to actually do something about it. It became real. I saw that the problem did exist. Admitting it to God helped me see the reality of the situation and gave me strength to deal with it.

Admitting the problem to Cathy also made it easier for me to begin to deal with it. Stating it to another person and promising to deal with it has more power than merely acknowledging it to oneself. I found myself compelled to take action because I had openly taken the responsibility and had promised to try. It made a difference. This shortcoming, as well as many others, still surfaces from time to time, but since I recognize its existence I am better able to handle it realistically and thus make progress.

There are good reasons why we should admit the nature of our wrongs not only to ourselves but also to another human being and to God. You ask, "Why must we admit our shortcomings to God? Doesn't he already know them?" This is a valid question. God does know us—better than we know ourselves. He knows all of our shortcomings well, but if we don't acknowledge these shortcomings personally and take responsibility for them, then God can't help us. He will not interfere with our freedom or take anything away from us that we do not acknowledge and consciously desire to remove.

We see this principle in many biblical stories. Why did God ask Adam and Eve what they had done after they ate the forbidden fruit? Didn't he already know? Of course he did, but God asked them so they would reflect on their actions and take the responsibility. Many times when Jesus healed someone of a sickness, he asked the sick person what he wanted. He even questioned those who were noticeably ill, "What do you want me to do for you?" or "Do you wish to be made well?" It makes little sense that Jesus asked these questions until we recognize that each of these people, on a spiritual level, represents us.

The word "Adam" means "man." A basic principle is expressed here that applies to Adam and Eve and also to each of us. The blind, the sick, and the lame symbolize ourselves in times of inner blindness, sickness, and infirmity. Jesus' healing of these people symbolizes the spiritual healings he performs on us. But before he can heal our spiritual infirmities, we have to recognize them, admit that we have a problem, and ask for help. That is how to open the way for his healing power. By confessing our shortcomings to God we are in effect saying, "God, I am blind; help me to see. I am sick; make me well. I am unable to live in your ways; help me that I might walk." Confession—inviting

God in to heal us—brings about union with God.

Admitting the nature of our wrongs to God and to ourselves gets us started on the path to spiritual growth. But we might wish to confess these things to another person. Why? Because it is an opportunity to bring our total personality into full light, giving us the most objective view of ourselves that we have ever encountered. Confessing to another human being forces us to take a hard look at our problems and gives a truly balanced picture of ourselves.

Often, after doing some hard soul-searching, we find ourselves becoming introverted and prone to isolating ourselves from others. Perhaps some of our problems make us feel we are worse than others. We may think our problems are so unique that no one else could understand them. We tend to deny some shortcomings and place too much stress on others. For example, we might consider a lack of initiative our biggest problem when, actually, it is an indifference toward others. Or introspection may suggest that a fear is our obstacle instead of a selfishness that holds us back.

When we risk opening our hidden selves to another, we are forced to acknowledge the effect our spiritual life has on others. No longer alienated from the human race, we relate our inner lives to that human race.

Beyond this, we see another human being respond to our problems with a different point of view and we become less myopic. There is comfort in knowing others who share similar shortcomings and can understand us, show compassion, and offer help.

A woman pointed this out to me. She always felt motherhood was her greatest problem. She believed she was a terrible mother to her three children because she yelled at them, didn't give them enough individual attention, neglected to teach them, and couldn't give them enough love. She knew other mothers who appeared to be "supermoms," doing everything right, creating a wonderful life for their children. Why couldn't she be more like them? Motherhood, or lack of it, topped her list of shortcomings.

When she finally reached Step Five and admitted her shortcomings to God, herself, and especially to another person, her perspective about her own motherhood changed. She went to a counselor who, having raised a family of her own, related a few of her own experiences and blunders as a mother. They laughed together that day and the woman began to admit that she really wasn't such a bad parent after all; after all, the counselor herself wasn't a perfect mother. Finally, the counselor shared an article on the foibles of parenting and recommended a support group for parents. The woman didn't join the support group, but after taking that fifth Step she felt better about herself. With a new resolve she began to tackle some of her parenting problems.

The support that comes from another is a boon not only to our spiritual life but also helps us to recognize our weaknesses. What we thought was a major problem might be minimized after discussion with a trusted person. On the other hand, what appear to be insignificant shortcomings may, in reality, need immediate attention. Talking about the specific problems can be therapeutic and enlightening. Often in this fifth Step the person who listens asks questions that clarify troublesome issues, help you face yourself honestly, and encourage you to make needed changes to achieve a better life.

If you are apprehensive about taking Step Five, perhaps my story will alleviate some of your fears and help you recognize the real benefits of this process.

I had taken a good personal inventory—about eighteen pages of notes. This is typical of one of my shortcomings; I tend to overdo everything. If the Step instructed me to be exact in my calculations then, by golly, I was going to be exact, and then some! I was eager to complete Step Five, admitting these shortcomings to God and to myself. But to talk to another person about my problems wasn't so easy. At that time, someone suggested that I seek out a professional—a minister, priest, psychologist, or counsellor—who was familiar with the Twelve Step Program. This is good advice, but don't consult someone you know well or see regularly. Go to a professional who is trained to offer objective, unbiased help.

I chose a highly recommended priest who had heard many fifth Step confessions. Already apprehensive, I found that his name offered little comfort: it was Father Scary. His name was appropriate for how I was feeling, but it didn't fit his character. He was open, warm, and a good listener.

As I began to express my shortcomings with a brief explanation of the more glaring ones, I felt naked, helpless, and vulnerable. It was not a comfortable feeling. I pictured him laughing uncontrollably, pointing at me, and saying, "You're a minister? Ha! Ha! Ha!... Your church is pretty desperate, huh? If you're the minister, I'd hate to meet the members of your congregation! Friends at the local clergy association are never going to believe this one when I tell them...."

Of course that didn't happen. Instead, he listened intently, and laughed and frowned with me but not at me. He added such phrases as "Gee, I remember when I did that," or "Gosh, you're making me feel bad. I still have a problem with that one." He also gave me advice here and there to help me overcome some of the problems. By the time I had my say I not only felt at ease; I felt wonderful. Not until I completed the fifth Step did I really understand what it was all about.

I walked out of the church with a new view of myself and a new resolve. I wasn't the worst person who ever lived nor was I the greatest. Neither was I special in any way: I had no major problems that others don't encounter from time to time. I had no powers or insights or abilities that exceeded the ordinary person. I discovered that I was "normal"—much like everyone else who makes mistakes from time to time, needs God's help, and has the potential to be a good person. But more than this, through the fifth Step I accepted responsibility for the flaws in my character and, in so doing, received the strength to deal with them. I left Father Scary with a new lease on life. No longer burdened with the baggage of guilt, fears, inhibitions, bad memories, and pain, I was invigorated with a new enthusiasm to carry me through the remaining Steps.

That is the beauty of the fifth Step. By accepting the responsibility for our shortcomings by confession before God, ourselves, and another human being, we let go of old hang-ups and become willing to start again. We see the potential for destruction in our lives, but we also see the potential for vast goodness, usefulness, fulfillment, and joy.

In taking the fifth Step we lay ourselves on the line. Confessing our shortcomings to another human being offers perspective and objectivity. Confessing them to ourselves helps us accept responsibility for them. Confessing them to God readies us to receive his help in removing them from our lives. We leave Step Five with new vision, but we will return to it from time to time as we change, grow, and discover even deeper parts of ourselves.

Once we were blind; now we see. Once we felt crippled and lame, now we find new strength and vitality to follow our God. With this new strength of purpose and vision we move forward with confidence and resolve to begin a new life.

TASKS: Learning to open oneself to God, to self, to others

1. Think about one destructive tendency within yourself that has occasionally harmed others. Go to a private place (e.g., your bedroom, bathroom, car) and say to God, "I admit I have a tendency to_____; it is a destructive tendency. Help me to recognize it."

2. Choose either the same or another destructive tendency, admit it to God, then find a mirror. Look into the mirror and say to yourself, "I confess that I have a tendency to_____and that it is hurtful to others. I have confessed this to God and to myself and am ready to begin to face this problem."

3. Find someone you trust and share with them a minor transgression you have committed lately. Notice how you feel.

(Tasks 1, 2, and 3 are a sampling of how to work Step Five. If you're really serious about spiritual growth, take your inventory to a professional and let it all hang out!)

Step Six

"Became entirely ready to have God remove all these defects of character."

We have come a long way. Working through the first five Steps, we have made many discoveries about ourselves. We have seen good things and have recognized flaws. We are aware of the vast potential for spiritual growth, but at the same time recognize destructive tendencies that could lead to disaster. We have acknowledged these tendencies and the consequent actions that bring hurt to ourselves and others. We have admitted this before God and another human being. In Step Six, we prepare to remove these defects of character and begin a new life.

A positive process

Focusing on our character defects, admitting them, and then asking God to remove them from us may appear to be a negative process. People who have not encountered or worked with the Twelve Steps ask about their negative aspect.

These Steps are really not negative. Quite the contrary; they are truly positive. This becomes evident when one begins to work them. We return to the analogy that our lives are like a garden with many beautiful flowers as well as many noxious weeds. Is weeding that garden a positive or a negative process? It may be a difficult and tedious task with a short-term focus on the bad, but the end result is a positive one. A gardener removes the weeds and the garden flourishes.

And what about the company that finds a defect on the production line? Is it a negative action to locate the defect and then fix it? There is, of course, a time of analysis with a focus on a specific problem, but this is only temporary until the problem is resolved and the company resumes production.

What if we are suffering from cancer? Is it a negative process to diagnose it, isolate it, and then remove it? Obviously, it is a positive procedure. So it is with our spiritual growth. It may be difficult—even painful—to recognize defects, admit them, and remove them from our lives, but the end result is a beautiful, blossoming life. We become good, useful, and spiritually healthy human beings. Nothing is more positive than that.

A priority in spiritual growth should be to rid oneself of shortcomings. This takes precedence over prayer, meditation, good deeds, reconciliation, everything! Why? Because for every character defect we remove, its opposite—virtue—takes its place. Think about that. Take away hate and love replaces it. Take away greed and benevolence takes its place. Take away pride and humility takes its place. Take away disorder and order takes its place. Becoming ready to have God remove these defects of character and actually having them removed is the crux of this Twelve Step Program. When we remove hate, pride, greed, and disorder, God takes their place for God is goodness, love, benevolence, and order. When we remove these, God's very nature replaces them for this is how God enters into us and affects us.

Sometimes we think of God as a self-contained entity with no relationship to us except that he created us, deposited us in the world, and tells us how to live. We often experience God as an obscure, elusive being. Contrariwise, God really is love and when love enters our hearts we allow God to enter. God is peace, joy, and serenity. Every good we experience mirrors God within us. We are not God, but God can dwell with us and within us. "Behold I stand at the door and knock. If any man hear my voice and open the door, I will come into him and sup with him and he with me" (Rv 3:20) bears this out. How essential it is, then, to remove those things which are contrary to God so God can replace them.

Becoming entirely ready

Steps Six and Seven—becoming ready to remove these defects and then asking God to remove them—are closely related. One might even wonder why a Step for getting ready is necessary. Can't we move directly to get rid of these character defects? No. This Step—getting ready to change—needs time; one must prepare for the changes to come. We want to be entirely ready for God to remove these defects of character, but that is not easy.

Why is this true? Because we are quite attached to many of these character defects. Of course, we are ready to shed those that cause us immediate pain, but we are less inclined to let go of those we are comfortable with. They are a part of us that gives delight. The delight may be a quick fix or a cheap thrill that ultimately leads to unhappiness, but we suffer from this insanity occasionally. We cling to things that are often bad for us. Asking God to remove some shortcomings may be easy but others may be more difficult.

For instance, we recognize in ourselves the tendency to lord it over people at work. We act like the big shot, insisting that our way is the only way, never admitting mistakes, never giving others a break. We might want God to remove this defect since we sense that co-workers don't appreciate or like us very much. We've struggled with our own impertinence and know what an ass we can make of ourselves. We can say quite readily, "God, take this from me; I don't want to be like this anymore!" On the other hand, we may be less ready to deal with other shortcomings on the work front. We may have found an easy way to doctor our expense account and make a few extra dollars on the side. Having grown accustomed to spending this money, it's hard to give up this practice. We willingly give up the one shortcoming, but grudgingly forsake the other.

Perhaps we suffer from guilt, fear, or depression, and would gladly rid ourselves of these inadequacies. But we cling tenaciously to self-pity, self-centeredness, and contempt for others. To relinquish our hold on greed, hunger for power, or vindictiveness may be easier than letting go of sexual fantasies, manipulative practices, or a sense of self-importance. If we are truly serious about our spiritual growth, we must let go of all of our defects.

Sometimes we believe we're ready to give up certain shortcomings or at least their consequences, but we never attempt to deal with the actual problem. We work hard at changing the effects of the shortcomings but avoid the root of the problem.

For instance, consider a father who has an alcohol problem. He comes home drunk night after night. He can't carry on a normal conversation at the dinner table. He has only derogatory comments for his son. He asks, on cue every night, "Have you done your homework? Isn't it time for you to go to bed? What the hell are you doing watching TV if your homework isn't done!" Once in awhile, when he has really tied one on, he pulls out his belt and raps his son across the back of the legs to speed him into his bedroom. Other times, he's too hung over to attend his son's ball games or to work with the son on a project. By the time he feels good enough to get going again, he hits the bottle, then goes to the games loaded, loud, belligerent, making a fool of himself. Or he tries to help his son with a project and ends up ruining the whole thing.

When this father awakes, he knows the hell he is causing his family. The guilt and depression are enough to kill him. He cries because he's not the father his son should have. He decides he will change; he'll show his son that he is a good dad, that he cares. He begins a new life. Instead of coming home drunk and belligerent, he comes home drunk with a gift in his hand. He slaps his son on the back and says in a loud, slurred voice, "Here, son, I brought you a present. It's a new baseball glove." After dinner he insists that they play catch, but he can hardly stand up to go out the back door. Night after night he either brings his son a gift or drags him to a baseball game or bowling or to a movie. He even lets his son stay up late, with just a few subtle derogatory comments, and raises his son's allowance.

Perhaps the son will never dare say what he is thinking. If he could find the courage to talk to his dad, he would tell him how he feels and what he really wants. He might say, "Please, please listen to me. I don't want to stay up all night. I don't want your money. I don't want more baseball mitts or other stupid gifts. I don't like bowling; I'm tired of baseball games. I don't want to see any more movies. I just want my dad. I just want my dad!"

Alcoholics are good examples of people who work on the periphery of their lives, trying to change but never tackling the root of the problem. We all do this to some extent. We recognize a problem and decide to change. However, we work superficially and only on its effects; the cause remains untouched.

If we want spiritual growth, we can't do it half-heartedly. We have to give ourselves over completely to God. Not just one or two, but all defects must go. Unless we work wholeheartedly and sincerely at ridding ourselves of all shortcomings, our spiritual growth becomes a sham.

To illustrate why we need to let go of these destructive tendencies absolutely, let's personify them and call them Dr. Jekyll and Mr. Hyde. We may want to be Dr. Jekyll, but there is a Mr. Hyde in all of us. Mr. Hyde is the epitome of everything undesirable within us. He is not only responsible for our every character defect or destructive inclination, he is our character defect. If left to rule us, Mr. Hyde will lie, steal, or kill to get his way. He is not a nice guy and we'd like to get rid of him. We don't need him, for every time he emerges he works havoc in our lives.

How do we get rid of him? The Twelve Steps give the answer—a simple one. Recognize him, take responsibility for letting him come out from time to time, become ready to be rid of him, and pray to God to remove him. Sound simple? It is, and the wonderful thing is, it works! But it poses a problem: we have to *want* to remove him. You can't expel a part of him and still hold onto the other part. You can't say, "I'd like him to stop killing, but he can keep stealing." You can't say, "I no longer want him to fill me with fears, but if he wants to use people, that's fine." If we hold on to part of our destructive tendencies, we don't completely release the rest of them. It's like kicking Mr. Hyde out while we still cling to his coattails.

If we truly want spiritual growth and happiness in our lives, but renege and deal with only part of our problems, do we really change for the better? That's not likely. If we stop lording it over people but refuse to deal with our sense of pride, our pride will eventually lead us back to lording it over people. It's easy to deal with our deceitfulness but letting go of our greed poses a problem. Are we changing for the better or only lying to ourselves? The greed will lead us back to deceitfulness. If we ask God to remove our fears but refuse to let him touch our contempt for others, are we really dealing with the total destructive self within us? Are we growing spiritually?

None of these examples imply that putting more emphasis on one shortcoming over another necessarily impedes progress in others. We can weaken Mr. Hyde's power and make progress simply by dealing with any one of our shortcomings. Spiritual growth takes dedication, and we must be willing to go all the way. Do we want Mr. Hyde as our companion or do we want

God to change us? We can't have both.

Let's look at one more illustration. If we have cancer and God is our surgeon, can we say, "God, remove this portion of the cancer but don't touch the cancer growing in this other area." Perhaps God can come in where we let him, but sooner or later the untreated cancer will infiltrate and eventually kill the body. If spiritual growth is significant, then tell the Doctor, "Do what you gotta do," and let him take care of it.

Once we reach the decision to change, we turn ourselves over to God to do whatever he must to change us. We open the way for changes to take place and deal with one character defect at a time. One may take precedence over another. Some will re-emerge from time to time, but with a full commitment, we allow God to make changes wherever necessary.

How do we become entirely ready for God to remove our character defects? We simply do our best. We don't claim spiritual perfection, but we claim spiritual progress. This is important to remember. We can strive for perfection, but achieving it is an ideal. Only God is the perfect being. All we can do is try. We can be honest with ourselves, look at all facets of our life, and ready ourselves for God to work in us. If we are willing to cooperate with God in beginning a new life, then we are ready for Step Seven.

We may fear that if we let go of all these character defects, we may no longer feel like ourselves. We may fear that by making so many changes we will lose our sense of self. That's a risk we take. After taking that risk and working these Steps, we will recognize that this isn't true. We do not lose our sense of self. On the contrary, we gain more of a sense of self. The more we let God in to make the necessary changes, the more we will feel like ourselves, and this brings more happiness, contentment, and self-worth than we had ever dreamed possible.

I met a woman at a Twelve Step meeting who summed it up like this: "I don't know much, but I do know one thing. There is a God and it ain't me." That, my friend, is the beginning of wisdom. We may be afraid at times to let go of some things within us which seem to be a part of ourselves. But we don't need to be afraid. Trust in that higher Power. Give God a chance to do what is necessary for you to grow. You have nothing to lose and everything to gain.

TASKS: Loosening up to let God change you

1. Think of one character defect or shortcoming that you really don't want to let go. Analyze the reasons for your hesitancy. Determine how this particular defect hurts you.

2. On a specific day blot out one pet shortcoming. Examples: Try not to tell one lie; abstain from criticizing others. Was it easy? How can you make yourself ready to let God make those changes for you?

Step Seven

"Humbly asked Him to remove our shortcomings and began a new life."

Humility

Humility is essential for spiritual growth. We don't stand a chance at achieving any constructive spiritual change or growth without it. If we are full of self and our own self-importance, God cannot enter in; there is no room for him. When we become proud and egotistical, we fully believe we are the source of all our happiness, the master of our fate, the creator and redeemer of our own lives. With such an attitude, it doesn't take long for our spiritual lives—even our earthly lives—to come crashing down on us.

I once heard a remarkable man talk at an open AA meeting about humility and how he came to know it firsthand. He was a stockbroker and a recovering alcoholic. He admitted that, before he found AA and the Twelve Step Program, he was probably the most egotistical person anywhere. He entered the world of stocks and bonds just as the market was taking off on a slow climb to an all-time high.

During his drinking "career," he spent most of his time picking and choosing stocks on a drunken whim more than on any fact sheet or analysis. Like so many "charmed drunks," he was extremely lucky and couldn't lose money. Every stock he picked went up; as they went up his own sense of importance went up. At that time he believed himself to be the greatest and most successful broker in the country and that he would die a rich, famous man. Moreover, people treated him like a great oracle of old—associates, friends, even his boss came to him for counsel. He was given responsibility for the largest accounts in the company and this whiz-kid of Wall Street doubled and tripled its money.

As he escalated to the top, he bought a mansion with a pool, two new cars, and everything less affluent people only dream about.

Every night his mansion turned into a party palace where he hosted a grand victory celebration of the champion he surely was.

During one of these parties, after he had six or seven cocktails, the president of a foreign oil company phoned him, quite upset upon hearing news about a certain stock that this broker had bought for the company. It seems the news could make a large difference in this oil company's assets, making or break the company. The broker was so drunk that he could understand only a few sentences the executive, with his foreign accent, was speaking. He did hear the man say repeatedly, "Should we buy more or sell? Should we buy or should we sell?" The broker, wanting to get back to the party, simply put the phone to his chest, hesitated, then came back to the phone and said, "Sell." He hung up and went back to the party.

When the stockbroker told this story he admitted that he could just as easily have said "Buy." He had kept hearing buy or sell, buy or sell. "I guess the last word I heard was 'sell' so I said 'sell.' " The next day the stock plummeted. His client could have lost a fortune; the man called him later, almost in tears. He praised the broker and kept saying, "Thank God. Thank God." Finally, the broker, in a wave of egomania said, "God? Thank God? Don't thank God! Thank me!" This was the peak of his arrogance. "Don't thank God! Thank me!" He thought he was God.

What happened next is typical when people begin to think they really are God and that nothing can shatter their omnipotent reign of glory. The broker made a bad selection in stocks—and then another and another and still another. Then the market crashed and he hit bottom in a matter of weeks. At the same time, he came to the realization that he was not only an alcoholic who desperately needed help, but he was nothing at all without God. Only God could bring him back to sanity and a balanced picture of himself and his life.

Today he is an average broker, but one who is happy for the first time and is making it in life. He admits he has something far more valuable than monetary wealth. He has humility.

I don't feel sorry for this man and the mistakes he made, but his story illustrates what pride and conceit can do. They blind us to the truth about our selves and life. They cause us to make incredible mistakes. They put us in the place of God, blocking him so completely out of our life that he cannot possibly help us or change us. Perhaps the only thing that helped this man spiritually was to lose the whole world to gain his own soul.

If we have sincerely taken Step One of this program, our inward lives will have little in common with that stockbroker and his ordeal. But during the course of working these Steps we need to consciously keep a humble heart. If we don't, we will overlook some of our more critical character defects. When we begin the process of asking God to change us, we won't let him make the changes. We'll try to make the changes ourselves without his help, and the result will be nil. We need God; we need to recognize that we need God. Without that recognition, we're back to square one.

I listened to a young man at a Twelve Step meeting explain that he was ready to confront any character defect in himself, but that he had one problem: he didn't see any character defects. I laughed at his naivete, knowing full well that when he began to work seriously on doing an inventory he would discover some defects and soon change his tune. I also noticed his lack of humility. That one defect was blinding him from seeing any others. He obviously was a novice to the Twelve Step Program.

If we have worked the first six Steps of this program faithfully, we will be humbled. We will know our powerlessness over the destructive tendencies within us. We will see how our sanity is challenged without a higher Power to guide us. Having let go of old ideas, we will have begun to listen to a higher Voice. Through a personal inventory and confession, we have identified our character defects and have taken measures to work on removing those defects. We know humility.

Humility is used in this Step to remind us that we will still be tempted to tackle these character defects alone—without God's help. However, as we have seen in Step One, we don't have the power to deal on our own with these destructive tendencies. We can fight against them, but we can't beat them. Not until we allow God to fight the battle for us and change our hearts will victory over these destructive tendencies come our way.

Cooperating with God

Asking God to remove our shortcomings isn't enough. We have to do our part and cooperate with God to allow these changes to take place. The all-powerful God makes the changes, but we allow him to make them through our actions. At times it may seem we are acting by ourselves yet we fully recognize that God is making the changes within us.

To strengthen this concept, call to mind an alcoholic who, drink in hand and between gulps, asks God to stop him. Or consider how many people with uncontrollable appetites have stuffed their faces with the third pizza, paused for a moment, and asked God to stop them from eating so much? People who suffer from these compulsions will admit that it happens, but God can't help them until they begin to help themselves. The alcoholic has to awaken in the morning and walk past that bottle on his way to get some help. The overeater has to learn a different behavior to deal with his compulsion. God gives these people the power to change their actions and takes away the defect, but they must act in cooperation with him.

Not all people familiar with the Twelve Step Program agree that we have to act as if by ourselves to remove shortcomings. Some argue that we don't play any part in removing character defects except in asking God to remove them. To ask God for help, they say, and then to do it oneself is like telling someone to park your car, then grabbing the keys and parking it yourself. Proponents of this view argue that you have to let God do it all.

I question this attitude. If God really wants to do it all, then I dare anyone to go to the passenger side of their car, hold up the keys, and ask God to drive you to your destination. Wouldn't that be silly? God doesn't want to drive the car. God didn't create you so that he could take away all the fun or do all the work. He wants you to drive, but he wants to guide you. He wants to lead you in the right direction, along the best path, but he doesn't want to take over. God created us with the feeling of self-life, the feeling of our own sense of power, the feeling of joy in living and acting as we please. He gave us these feelings so we can freely choose to allow his love to guide and touch us deeply and then we, in turn, can freely touch others with his love as if it were our own. It is God's love and very life which affect us. But we make the choices; we do the actions. By this means, we make that love and life our own.

We can see illustrated in many Bible stories this principle of cooperating with God. In Step Three we talked about the story of

Peter walking on the water. Indeed, it was God's power holding Peter up and allowing him to walk on the stormy water, but Peter still had to walk. In the same way, it is God's power which holds us up when we call upon him during the storms we encounter, but we still have to do the walking; that is, living the best we know how.

Many people that Jesus or one of the prophets healed were told to get up and walk or to go and wash in a pool or in the Jordan River. These healings, as we have seen, represent the spiritual healings God performs. If we want to be healed, we can't just sit and wait for miracles. We have to get up and get out of our state of disorder. We have to wash and be clean. Isn't that what the prophet's words meant: "Wash yourselves, make yourselves clean. Put away the evil of your doings. Though your sins be as scarlet they shall be as white as snow." When Naaman, the Syrian leper, was told to go and wash in the Jordan River to be cleansed of his leprosy, it was, indeed, God who healed him, but Naaman still had to wash. In the same way, we have to wash; we have to put away our character defects as if the effort were ours alone while, realizing at the same time, that God actually removes them and heals us. God makes us whole.

One defect at a time

When we humbly ask God to remove our defects of character, we should be specific. To begin this Step, find a quiet place to be alone, list those defects, and make a vocal prayer for help. We may ask God to remove our anger, our stubbornness, our self-pity, our lust, and every defect within ourselves. But after a general appeal, we select one or two defects that need special attention. We will work in cooperation with God to help rid us of these problems. After we make progress in these areas, we move on to one or two more shortcomings. We will continue this process throughout our lives and as we remove each character defect, we will become better and more spiritual persons.

Why deal with one or two shortcomings at a time? Because we must focus on specifics if we really want God to remove defects. If we don't, we will be making a general plea to change without concentrating on what specifically needs changing. Besides, we are not capable of handling all shortcomings at once.

Let's face it; if we are honest in our inventory, we probably have a list of ten, twenty, or even thirty shortcomings. We simply can't focus on all of them simultaneously. It could be depressing to focus on even four or five.

Imagine praying: "God, take away my anger, my stubbornness, my insecurity, my fears, my lusts, my envy, my insincerity, my hunger for power, my laziness, my self-pity, my this, my that." Why not just say, "God, take away my character defects. Thank you very much." A prayer like this would be useless. If we need only say, "God, take away my defects," then why take an inventory to discover these defects? To reiterate, we take the inventory and then ask God to remove specifically one or two shortcomings at a time; we focus on them and work in cooperation with God for their removal. The saying, "One day at a time" is apropos here if we change one word: "One *defect* at a time."

The defects an individual chooses to remove are a personal decision. At the outset, we may choose a defect or two that we can possibly remove with ease, or we might work at a bad habit or a fear. After removing these, we will be more confident and can advance to more difficult inbred character defects. On the other hand, we may initially choose to deal head-on with the defects that cause the most trouble. Perhaps we're at the end of our rope, dragged around by an inbred lust for pleasure or by a fiery temper that flares up to cause family suffering. These may be extremely difficult character defects, but we choose to tackle them first because they are the most destructive. Again, the choice is an individual one.

Do not be discouraged

When we begin this process—asking God to remove our defects of character—we may be surprised at how easily we shed some of them, never to see them again because they were minor and played an insignificant role in our lives. All we needed was a simple prayer to release them. Others, however, may be more difficult and put up a good fight. Don't be discouraged. Always bear in mind that we cannot expect spiritual perfection, only spiritual progress.

If God is really all loving and all powerful, why doesn't he remove all of these defects when we ask him? Why do some linger and continue to give trouble? They stay because we don't completely let go of them. Something inside us continues to hold on and we have to work hard to discover that. There can be a lot of pain before we recognize fully and completely that we are holding on to some defects that we don't want to hold on to any longer.

God isn't going to take anything from us that we really haven't given up. Our freedom is important—to God and to us. We may be holding on to some inner garbage; we ask God to take it from us, but when he reaches out to take it, we subconsciously pull away and clutch it close to our being. We are not ready to let it go. God is waiting to aid us, but we have to accept that aid.

A person may recognize he has a real problem with depression. He keeps sinking into self-pity. Family pressures, problems at work, life in general release this "pity me" posture. At times, he may acknowledge the self-pity to himself and to others. He even asks God to remove it from him—and his spirits lift. Life seems better and it's fairly easy to keep his mind off himself and to concentrate more on his family or his tasks at work. Eventually, however, this inner feeling of self-pity resurfaces. This feeling is alluring. He toys with it and spends time counting his woes. At other times he rejects the feeling and makes an effort to forget about himself and get on with life. Nevertheless, it becomes more and more difficult to shrug off the self-pity until, finally, one day when things go wrong—his work load is heavy or he's had an argument with his wife—he complains "Why me?" He sits at his desk lamenting his bad breaks: "Why does God put me through all this? Why are people so rotten to me? What's the use?" Eventually, the man finds himself where he started, wallowing in his own self-pity.

Why is the man's character defect so tenacious? Is it because his life is pervasively evil or because God refuses to take it from him? Is it because the defect is too powerful for him to handle? No. It remains a problem because he never lets it go completely. He prefers to feel sorry for himself again, to hold onto a part of the defect—and so it resurfaces in full form. It will continue to recur until he decides to fully let go.

A good friend of mine—a recovering alcoholic—told me his story; it helps illustrate this point. He said he had tried many,

many times to stop drinking but just couldn't seem to do it. He'd get help and get sober. Then he'd get adventuresome and head off to a friend's party or a card game with the boys. As he drove to his friend's house, he prayed, "Please, God, help me not to drink. Please help me not to drink." But it never worked. He'd arrive there and eventually get loaded.

Not until his third attempt did he finally lick the problem. He was taking the usual course: Invited to a party, he hopped into his car and headed down the street. As he approached his friend's house, he started thinking about what he was doing. He soon felt his powerlessness over the situation. He didn't want to drink that night, but he didn't know how he could stop himself. In desperation he prayed aloud, "God, don't just help me not to drink. Make me so I won't drink! Please make me stop." A voice from within responded immediately. It said quite strongly, "Turn the car around! Turn it around right now!" And he felt the power to do that. He turned the car around and went home. Today, he avoids those parties at all cost and has been sober for about two years.

Obviously, my friend should have known he couldn't associate with the same crowd. But look deeper into the problem. In the beginning, attempting to stay sober, he never really turned the problem over to God. He'd ask God to help, but he wouldn't let God in. God had not been silent on this issue nor did he refuse to deal with the man until he begged for help. God was there each time he headed toward another party, saying quite strongly, "Turn the car around." But he wasn't listening. It was only when he felt complete powerlessness over the situation and let go that he heard God's voice and allowed God's power to give him the strength to turn around and go home. Finally, he not only had new power to deal with the problem, but he was also enlightened. My friend realized that within his desire to go to these parties was hidden a desire to keep drinking. He hadn't really let it go until he reached that final state of desperation and prayed to God not only to help him but also to make him stop.

So it is with any of us. It will not always be easy to allow God to remove our character defects, but at those times when we wonder why God has not taken them away, we must take a good, hard look at ourselves. What are we holding onto? When we determine that, we must let go. Every time we resist one defect, we make progress. Eventually, when we are freed from them, we will be blessed with a new life.

A new life

That is the beauty of this Step; we do make real progress. Even those character defects which seemed to manipulate and ruin our lives are taken away. We may have struggled for years from certain fears, but after surrendering the fears to God they are gone and the discomfort in the stomach or chest is no more. We are healed! Anger, resentment, and jealousy may have plagued us. It is a tough battle, but after a time we learn to relinquish the hold on those negative feelings and our lives change. We no longer get angry; the resentment or jealousy is replaced with concern for others as well as a genuine belief in ourselves and our own worth. Old habits that may have seemed impossible to eradicate vanish once we've learned to turn them over to God. Truly, a new life has begun.

That is the last part of this Step—to begin a new life. As we allow God, with our cooperation, to remove our shortcomings, he opens up a new life for us. We have to be willing to start again in all facets of our lives and to leave the past behind. In this Step we let go not only of our character defects but also of our past and our memories of whom we might have been. We start anew.

Perhaps we had an unhappy childhood; memories may still be affecting our view of life. Perhaps we suffer from guilt and find it difficult to forget something we did five, ten, even fifteen years ago. We carry that "baggage" around in an attempt to make up for past mistakes. Let go! Take responsibility for the wrongs, right them, and make amends wherever possible. But don't carry the guilt. Forget the past; begin a new life. Jesus said, "Let the dead bury the dead." The past is dead. The past is gone. We are who we are now and won't be the same person even tomorrow. We must be reborn completely. The old person must die so the new person can be born.

"Today is the first day of the rest of your life." That sounds trite, yet it is true. Think about it. Say to yourself, "Nothing in the past has to affect me. I am not the person I used to be; I can begin again. I can be born anew. I can live for the first time—really live!"

The more we work Step Seven the more we grow spiritually. There is a new life and new healing. Like a cripple who takes up his bed and walks, we too can leave our infirmity behind and walk in ways of happiness and peace. Like a blind man who receives sight, we will see beautiful visions for the first time and behold the true beauty of this world, not just in nature but in relationships, in the face of a friend and in a child's smile. We may have been deaf to an inner guidance, but now we hear a gentle voice within, leading us, guiding us, and comforting us with tender care. Like a leper healed of his numbing disease, we begin to sense the joy of life. Inner numbness departs. Emotions well up within us that may be hard to control. Nevertheless, we feel vibrant, inwardly clean, and called forth to a new life. The old person has died; we are now born anew!

TASKS: Allowing improvements

1. Pick one shortcoming you've been pondering. Vocally, ask God to remove it, then stop doing it as if by your own power. What happens? Is this easier than when you did this same thing in Step Three? If not, why not? If so, why?

2. When you suspect you are in a negative state, notice the enjoyment you may be having from it. What is the payoff for the negative state? What negative delight is blocking higher enjoyment? Let go of the negative and allow the positive to take its place.

Step Eight

"Made a list of all the persons we had harmed and became willing to make amends to them all."

The need for this Step is evident in a Twelve Step Program for the recovering alcoholic. Anyone alcoholism has affected knows the damage that comes from this disease. The alcoholic might have harmed many people, and so needs to make amends. But the basic principles in this Step are important for anyone wanting spiritual growth. We may have many names on the list of persons we've injured, while others may not have any. Most of us, however, can bring to mind a few people we have harmed in one way or another and can right wrongs and make amends.

This Step dovetails with Step Seven. Making a list of the people we have harmed and then making amends help us to clear the slate, dump the guilt, and begin a new life. Who have we hurt in the past? Possibly we lashed out at someone with cruel words and accusations. Or in a selfish way we cheated someone and now regret it. Maybe we actually hurt someone physically by accident—but we've never resolved the guilt. Memories can haunt us and cling to us like leeches. If it is possible to right the wrongs, then we have golden opportunities to repair the damage and let go of the guilt. With a clear conscience, we can work toward a useful and constructive life that let's us see ourselves and our relationships with others in a new light.

Making amends also helps us turn good intentions into action and dreams into reality. Heretofore, we have been focusing mainly on ourselves. This, of course, is good and necessary. It's important to get our own act together before we can change our attitude toward others. Now we reach the point where we change our focus from looking inward to looking outward.

It's possible that we become so wrapped up and concerned with our own spiritual growth that we forget other people. For instance, we could say to someone close to us, "Will you stop bothering me? I'm too busy trying to be a spiritual person to be concerned with you right now." Of course, we wouldn't say that, but we can feel that way at times. In an attempt to feel good and more spiritual, we may run roughshod over others. Also, in working the first seven Steps we will experience great joy at the changes taking place within. Our enthusiasm to continue the quest may cause loved ones to feel left behind and perplexed at our behavior. If this happens we've missed the point in our quest for spirituality.

Making a list of those we have injured brings us back to reality. It's a reminder that we have some past hurts that need mending. It forces us to show concern for others. When we list the names of people we have harmed, what we have done to them, and how to make amends, we begin to see how we affect other people. We see the harm we have caused but also recognize the potential for good we can have on others. We create the opportunity to live constructively instead of destructively. We rebuild for ourselves and others the bridges we had wrecked in the past. We cross those bridges and look into the hearts of others, concerned with their concerns. We begin to love and to bring that love into life.

Codependency

Step Eight helps us build relationships. But often some of our past relationships need to be reordered before they can be rebuilt. Many people suffer from codependency. (A codependent is one who is addicted to a sick relationship much like an alcoholic is addicted to alcohol.) People who suffer from codependency usually come from dysfunctional families. The spouse of an alcoholic may often be as sick, even sicker, than the alcoholic. The root of the problem may lie in the alcoholism, but the spouse living with the diseased person for years may subconsciously learn sick patterns of thought and behavior which not only enable the alcoholic but also give the codependent a "fix."

A good example of this is the wife of an alcoholic who finds herself completely wrapped up in her husband's addiction. She sets herself up as the caretaker in the relationship, making sure others do not discover her husband's disease. She lies to his boss with the excuse that her husband is sick when, actually, he is hung over. She cleans up after his drunken excursions, supports his denials of disorder, and even becomes his supplier by seeing that the home is always stocked with alcohol in case of emergencies such as days when bars are closed.

Surprisingly, the wife can detest the alcoholism yet continue to enable it. In these situations, the wife plays the martyr. She believes she must carry the burden of the entire family, of home management, and financial responsibilities. Frequently, she becomes obsessed with her husband's addiction. He becomes the target of her anger and resentment, yet she hinges her sense of happiness and well-being on his behavior rather than on her own. She may moan and groan over her hopeless condition, but unwittingly continues to support the problem. She becomes addicted to the status quo and to feeling self-important by playing the martyr and the caretaker. She is addicted to the sick relationship.

It is not unusual, then, that many alcoholic marriages end in divorce, not while the alcoholic is drinking but after he gets help. Working through the Twelve Step Program of AA, the spouse wakes up spiritually, wants to take back from his wife those responsibilities he feels are rightfully his. He finds he is not as dependent on her as he once was and is ready to start again. Many times the wife can't tolerate this. She has become so addicted to the sick relationship of being in charge, being responsible, being the martyr, that her sick sense of self-esteem is thrown into turmoil because of his new sobriety. That is why Al-Anon was created. It not only helps those who live with a drunk but also helps those who live with a recovering alcoholic learn to recover themselves.

Codependency is not exclusive to alcoholism, yet it most often shows itself there. Many other people find themselves in sick relationships. They put all their sense of self-worth into what others think about them and how others treat them. Some people find themselves addicted to relationships which bruise them badly, not only mentally and emotionally, but also physically.

Making amends does not mean continuing to be a codependent nor does it mean turning the other cheek and becoming a slave to another's approval, behavior, addictive personality, or character disorder. Now and then, making amends means simply saying "No!"

The purpose of Steps Eight and Nine is to right the wrong and begin anew in relationships. Often, righting a wrong takes only a kind heart to accomplish reconciliation. Yet righting wrongs can also mean escaping a sick relationship by relying on your own initiative, learning to be your own person and then showing love and compassion to others. A wife who stops enabling her alcoholic husband is showing him far more love than one who fulfills his every whim. A person who terminates an unhealthy dependence on a friend is expressing more love for the friend than by remaining in the sick relationship and allowing that friend to use him. Sick relationships need not be broken and abandoned; they do, however, need to be rebuilt. It may be necessary to show tough love for a while and to separate long enough to find independence—and true love.

When I went to a Twelve Step group for codependents the first time, a woman who was introducing newcomers to the program told her story. It is a good illustration of the points above.

She had been in a sick relationship with her husband for over twenty years. Her marriage was always in turmoil because she was completely wrapped up in her husband's behavior, obsessed with his actions to the point of preparing for divorce. It wasn't until he was diagnosed as having a terminal disease that she felt she must turn somewhere for help in learning to cope with him under these new and stressful circumstances. When she learned about codependency, how to detach and deal with her own problems rather than her husband's, she then began to truly love him. Before that time she had focused her attention on his problems because she was afraid to face her own. After learning about codependency, she began to face these problems and to break away from the sick dependence she had on her husband. She held her ground and demanded dignity and respect from him. "As I began to see myself for what I really was, no longer dependent on my husband for happiness," she said, "I began to truly love him and to care for him in his condition.... We are lovers now, not necessarily in a physical sense, but deep within. He always thought he loved me, but I know that not until now did I really love him—and in a healthy way. I am not going to divorce him. I want to make his last days as warm and loving as possible."

When we reflect on the relationships we have built—the people we affect deeply and those who deeply affect us—we should look for those we have harmed and be willing to make amends. But we also should look for those relationships which harm us, be willing to break them down, and rebuild them. This is loving—a loving that leads to good and healthy relationships. This approach is also part of Steps Eight and Nine.

Make a list

How do we complete Step Eight? Set aside a block of time to reflect on your relationships, on your misdeeds, and on those you have harmed by them. Make a list of the relationships, the misdeeds, the names of the persons you hurt, and an idea or two on how to make amends. You might keep the list nearby for a few days should you want to add to it. When you have completed the list, you are ready for action.

Step Eight ends by saying we must be willing to make amends to all. This takes courage. We can easily approach some people, and right the wrongs we have done them. Others, however, we have perhaps vowed never to see again. Similarly, we can atone for some of our bad deeds without much of a problem, but others may cause real shame and embarrassment. Nevertheless, we have to deal with them if we want to bury the past and begin a new life. This may be a long and difficult task, but we must be willing to make amends to all.

This action demands a great deal of reflection on why we should do it, how best to do it, and when to do it. Sometimes immediate action is the best way. We must simply say to ourselves, "I'm scared to death, but I will do this." Then we jump in and do our best.

Have you ever had the experience of being really hot and then had the opportunity to jump into a cool, refreshing pool or lake? The cold water will be welcome but you still hesitate because of the initial shock. If you delay too long, you may never take the plunge and enjoy the water. The best thing to do is simply to jump. Some people rub water on their bodies and their heads and go through a torturous process of getting used to it. Even that is better than standing in the boiling heat, thinking how much you'd like to be refreshed, but holding back in anxiety about the first few cold and uncomfortable seconds.

A willingness to make amends is much the same. You'll feel

refreshed when you have completed your mission, but if you dillydally around and concentrate on the moments of initial discomfort, you'll never do it. So it's best to simply jump in. The outcome is worth it.

TASKS: Beginning that list

1. Make a list of five people you have harmed.
2. Write down an idea or two about how you might best make amends.

Step Nine

"Began to make amends, to do good, to be honest and faithful in all our affairs, and to walk humbly with our God."

Making amends

When we actually begin to make amends to those we have harmed, our primary goal is reconciliation. That is, we resolve the wrongs and the ill will, and mend the broken relationships. With reconciliation, we leave the past and start life and relationships anew in a productive manner.

Amends may be as simple as a sincere apology via a visit, a phone call, or a letter. Circumstances govern the approach. The first time I took Step Nine I gave a verbal apology to one person and a written one to another.

About six months before coming into contact with the Twelve Steps, I had lied to an associate who questioned me about a group of teenage kids who were drinking in the park. Their drinking was especially disturbing to the teacher since he had cautioned them about teenage drinking. I wasn't actually with the group, but I had talked to them for about fifteen minutes the night they were in the park. Weak-kneed, I told my associate I hadn't seen anyone. Why? Possibly because I didn't want to implicate anyone or maybe it was just easier to stay out of it. Regardless, he returned to my office later and said, "If you didn't see the kids, why did they say they saw you and spent some time talking with you?" Flushed from embarrassment, I mumbled something but stuck to my story.

As I was taking my Ninth Step six months later, I walked into his office and told him the truth. Indeed, I had lied. I apologized for such a stupid move and asked him to forgive me. He laughed and started recounting stupid things he had done as a teacher. We are now good friends.

My other apology was in a letter. I have yet to talk about my misdeed face to face with this person. We were good friends when I was in college and theological school. That was before I learned about the Twelve Steps, and I had some serious problems: I saw life in two colors—black and white—and two ways—right and wrong. My friend made a few ethical mistakes, mistakes that anyone can make from time to time. But as a young, idealistic, not too realistic or compassionate theological student, I saw only the wrong. When my friend faltered, I got out the cannon and fired the big one. I called the person evil, selfish, a devil, a mere semblance of a human being, and more! I cut all ties and walked away. Believe me, it made an impression.

It took almost five years and a move eight hundred miles away before I finally wrote a short letter of apology saying simply that I was wrong and that I hoped my friend would forgive me. I have not received a reply to that letter, but I don't deserve one. That is not the focus of this Step. The focus lies in my attempt to right the wrong, clear the slate, and start again. And I feel better about it. I know that I am forgiven—at least by God and myself.

Sometimes making amends does not center on apology and reconciliation. Perhaps it requires repayment for a debt or doing anonymously a good deed for someone. There is great opportunity for creativity in this Step, but we must be sincere, actually right the wrong, and make amends in the best way possible.

At one time you may have dipped into your company's expense account. Now you have the company on your list for making amends. Obviously, you don't want to walk into the boss's office and apologize for ripping off the company for the last twelve years. But you can make amends by replacing the money in a petty cash fund available to you without being obvious about it. Use your creativity. Deliver mysterious envelopes containing cash donations to your boss's desk. Work overtime without remuneration. You can usually find ways to make amends without being noticed.

There are times when a person may, for good reasons, want anonymity. For example, it would be imprudent—even destructive—to tell someone about an affair you had with their spouse years ago. What good would such a confession do? To make amends in this and similar circumstances is to terminate the wrong doing. Don't ruin another person's life simply to make yourself feel better. Make amends only when the action would not harm self or others.

Use good judgment in making amends. Seriously consider the best way to go about it and be completely honest about the motives for making amends. By apologizing, do we hope for an apology from the person we are in discord with? Are we making an appointment to see that person under the pretense of making an apology when we are actually planning to lay out all our resentments and unload on him or her? It's easy to do. We may say something like, "I'm really sorry I left you and the kids, but you were a real witch. I'm sure you're a lot different now," or "I'm sorry I didn't pay back the loan, but at the time I thought you were one of the stingiest people I'd ever known." That is not working the Ninth Step. We make amends to right wrongs, to do away with the negative, concentrate on the positive, and come to reconciliation. Most of the time the only words we need are, "I'm sorry." They may not say it all, but often they say enough.

Life is more than apologies

People familiar with the original Twelve Steps of AA will recognize that this Step reads differently from the original. For this book, Step Nine says, "Began to make amends, to do good, to be honest and faithful in all our affairs, and to walk humbly with our God." AA's Ninth Step says, "Made direct amends to such people wherever possible, except when to do so would injure them or others." For some who belong to AA, changing this or any Step might seem as unthinkable as altering the Ten Commandments. But keep in mind that the Twelve Steps were designed originally and specifically to help the recovering alcoholic. They were not designed for everyone.

As a program for the recovering alcoholic, the Twelve Steps of AA should probably never be changed. They are the alcoholic's "Ten Commandments" for sobriety. Recovering alcoholics usually must make amends for abuses which coexisted with the alcoholism. The Twelve Steps for Spiritual Growth, however, are not limited to the alcoholic; they are for everyone.

The spiritual life is more than a life of apologies. It is more than recounting repeatedly what a terrible person we've been and how much better we now are. The spiritual life is a positive life when we cease hurting others, make amends, and go forward to a life of goodness, honesty, joy, and love. That is why Step Nine of the Twelve Steps for Spiritual Growth tells us to go forward in life and "do good, be honest and faithful in all our affairs, and walk humbly with our God." It launches us into the full and satisfying life that is readily available.

Good deeds bring joy. When we learn to love others, we are blessed with all that is meaningful, fulfilling, and beautiful. Goodness and happiness are synonymous.

Jesus said, "Give and it will be given unto you." Does this mean that if we shell out now, we'll cash in on some great reward in heaven? Didn't Jesus also say, "The Kingdom of God is within you"? I strongly believe in the concept of heaven, but we begin to build that heaven within ourselves here on earth. The reward of a good life is the sheer joy that it brings. Essentially, that is what heaven is all about: goodness, love, happiness, and joy. Why wait? We can have that here to the degree that we give.

Think about a special time in your life when your whole being was filled with joy, if only for a brief moment. What was at the core of the experience? I think it was love, that desire to be close to another; love, the flame that warms another; love, the magnetic force that pulls you closer to another human being in an effort to become one; love, the force within that does good without thought of reward. Love gives hope and love brings joy.

Most parents try to make their children's lives happy lives. In my relationship with my children, I am attuned to their ups and downs and try to strengthen their good feelings and alleviate the bad ones. I observe their states of happiness and discover that they are happiest when they express love, when they are giving, not receiving or taking. One doesn't quickly forget the face of a child who has made some special gift for another child. It beams with joy. When one child helps another child find his way or consoles her after a fall, a spirit of joy pervades the child. Moreover, parents experience the same kind of joy when they observe this gift of joy in their children. Parents rejoice when their child takes those first steps, says those first words, or brings home a prize from school for a job well done. Parents rejoice as their children grow into young men and women who learn to think and act for themselves. There is, of course, a lot of pain in parenting. Nevertheless, the joy and pain merge into love to make it all worthwhile.

After we make amends, we go forth with new hearts on a journey of love. An adventure lies before us, and we experience a transformation of character. We find self-worth, contentment, companionship, and warmth. The journey is simple. We keep a cool head, do good wherever we can, live honestly, do our job faithfully, and walk hand in hand with God.

The spiritual life is not a complicated or grandiose scheme. We take life one day at a time, one obstacle at a time, one achievement at a time. That is why Step Nine tells us merely to act honestly and faithfully in our dealings with others and to be humble. If we keep a clear conscience and contain our ego, we will make progress. We won't set our expectations too high. We won't fill ourselves with guilt or remorse over failures or fill ourselves with pride and conceit over victories. God leads us every step of the way. If we remain humble, do the best we can, and hold God's hand, we will never be lost; we'll keep marching down that path toward spiritual success and prosperity.

TASKS: Working toward forgiveness and reconciliation

1. Select a person you have harmed in a small way; make amends verbally, openly, or covertly.

2. When a person offends you, ask God to forgive you for an offense against another. Place them side by side and note the difference. "Forgive us our trespasses *as* we forgive those who trespass against us."

3. When you feel regret or anxiety, observe a connection with the past. Let go and recall something positive in the here and now. Say to yourself, "This present moment is eternity; I am in the perfect place at the perfect time."

Step Ten

"Continued to take personal inventory and when we were wrong promptly admitted it."

Progress rather than perfection

Step Ten is the first step of the Twelve which indicates that spiritual growth and change are a process. Each day we move along the path we started. We continue with the personal inventory, keeping an eye on ourselves and our spiritual growth. We maintain a clear conscience and an open mind. And thus we continue to grow.

This is important. Some people believe that spiritual change and growth happen instantaneously, that there is not a progression. They assert that you need only confess your belief in a set of teachings and by that means you achieve spirituality. Granted, there may be a time when one "sees the light" and begins a conversion, but the battle for spiritual growth is not over. It has just begun. If a person believes he can do whatever he pleases because he is "saved," he is abusing, rather than using, a teaching. Yes, God forgives all, but if a person is unwilling to accept that forgiveness by amending his life, then that forgiveness doesn't do one whit of good.

It may be comforting to think that with a confession of belief we don't have to change, work, or grow. But, of course, this is a false notion. The problem with this belief is that closing our eyes to problems does not make them go away. How easy it would be to say a few magic words that would—presto!—change us into beautiful, spiritual people. But neither life nor human nature nor God works that way. Becoming a spiritual person is a lifelong process through day-by-day growth. We are not saints. We claim only spiritual progress, not spiritual perfection. Reality is hard to face. Our human nature doesn't want to deal with problems, but the sooner we confront them, the sooner we will know a genuine and fulfilling spirituality.

Old ways sometimes return

Step Ten helps to cultivate an awareness of life rather than to hide from it. This day-by-day Step helps our spiritual journey by advising us to keep eyes open to our spiritual growth and to recognize when old habits may be creeping in. Steps One through Nine help us recognize and remove destructive tendencies. Step Ten makes sure they don't become an active force once again.

Some old tendencies, though, do come back. In working the previous Steps we turn things over to God, start a new life, and make great spiritual strides and changes. We find, however, that bad habits and ways of thinking—once banished—do at times raise their ugly heads.

For instance, we might have let go of anger or resentment. Six months, maybe a year or two have passed and we haven't lost our temper or felt resentful. Then one day a co-worker really tests our patience. Perhaps we are teaching a person to do a job, and he keeps making the same mistake or goofs around and wastes time. Anger flares up and we yell and scold him for his ineptitude. Later, we ask ourselves, "Whoa, where did that come from? I thought I was rid of that."

These destructive tendencies can also resurface more subtly. We might have been quite the egotist, but the Twelve Steps helped to bring about a much more balanced, humble human being. Consequently, life in general has improved. When this happens, we may gradually forget about a higher Power and attribute our successes and triumphs to the fruit of our own labor and ignore the benefits of following a higher Power. We may take the credit for the good things we've accomplished in life and give little credit to God. Slowly the egotism begins to emerge, and we are again full of self and our own sense of importance, right where we started with this character defect.

We are asking valid questions: "Why do these destructive tendencies come back? Can we ever be rid of them completely?" The answer, of course, is that we never eradicate them completely. Like peeling an onion, we do away with one layer at a time. Sometimes we can get the feeling that the layers will never end. But each time we deal with them we take away some of their power and effect on our lives so that we can change dramatically for the better. By working the Twelve Steps—especially Step

Ten—these character defects can eventually be expelled.

An elderly woman once told me she had been working with this program for years. She was ninety-one years old, a sweet, angelic lady. When I asked her if she had always been so sweet, her reply surprised me. She said, "Sometimes I feel I've been working on the same shortcomings all of my life. I don't see much progress—only the same old problems."

How depressing! Had she really been working on these same problems all of her life? Had she made no progress? Everyone acquainted with her knew she had grown in her love, her charm, and her spirituality. One could sense this in a first meeting with her. However, she herself was unaware that her spiritual labors were not in vain but actually quite fruitful.

She had grown dramatically, but a perception of her personal shortcomings increased with that growth. So aware of them, she did not see the progress she had, indeed, made over them. This can happen to anyone who focuses on and struggles with character defects.

There are times when we need to take a good look at ourselves to see these changes. If we feel dismayed over our shortcomings, it is a signal to reflect on what life was like before we began our journey toward spiritual growth. It won't take long to recognize progress.

To illustrate, compare our spiritual program—the cleansing of character—to window washing. The windows are dirty and so badly smudged that we can hardly see through them. Before beginning the program we seemed to have little control over the situation. The dirty windows were bothersome; they blocked out the sunlight, but we had little initiative to wash them. There were too many and they were just too dirty.

Then begins our program for spiritual growth. We call on a greater Power to motivate us and to start on one window at a time. The room seems brighter with each washing. There are still a few smudges, though, that just don't seem to come off. We spend hours working to remove them. These few smudges trouble us a great deal. We focus on them, become dismayed over them. If only we could get rid of the darn smudges, the windows would be clean. We say, "I've been washing windows all of my life but this dirt is still here!"

How quickly we forget. Once the room was dark and gloomy;

now it is full of light. While it seems we have been doing the same job all along, things really have changed. Once we felt powerless over the dirt and we sat in the dark. Oddly enough, now the light pours in but we become concerned and weary over a few remaining marks on the pane. Again, we must step back and appraise our work. Yes, we have changed and grown and most of the dirt has been removed. We must simply recognize this fact.

The emergence of a particular shortcoming does not indicate a sign of spiritual digression nor does it mean we are faltering or going backward in our spiritual journey. Some shortcomings come back so we can deal with them on a deeper level.

Let's return to the garden analogy. The first time we deal with a specific shortcoming we merely chop off its head like a weed in the garden. The next time it appears, we cut it off at ground level. The third time it emerges we decide, "I'll get on my knees and dig the darn thing out." It disappears forever.

If the first time we faced that shortcoming we could see how ugly it really is, we'd be horrified. God lets us see only a little so we won't be afraid to tackle just a bit at a time. Had we seen the entire malignant problem immediately, we'd have said, "Why try? It's too much for me."

When you become dismayed about your spiritual growth because a shortcoming recurs, ask this simple question: "How do I feel about this?" Perhaps you were an egotist, or a drunk, or a harsh critic. If you are now concerned about it and see it as an enemy rather than as friend, then you have come a long way. Before you started down your spiritual path, how did you feel about that shortcoming? You loved it; it was part of you. You loved being an egotist. You loved getting bombed every day. You loved being critical of other people. These things were killing you, but they ruled your life. Now they no longer rule you. When they do come up, they become an intruding enemy to be squashed immediately. You've come a long way in your effort to change, and you are a completely different person.

Personal inventory

Step Ten allows us to continue on the path of change and growth. Continuing with a personal inventory makes it possible to detect destructive forces before they once again become an active force. By observing our behavior on a regular basis and getting to know ourselves better, we can, for example, see the potential for anger coming back, we can see the egotism before it becomes a ruling factor in our lives once again. Seeing these tendencies begin to surface, we can deal with them before they cause trouble. Like weeds growing in a garden, we nip them in the bud.

This personal inventory acts as a shield against the emergence of destructive tendencies. When we tend to be stubborn or angry or selfish, we anticipate them and can fend off their influence. Perhaps a voice from within tells us to retaliate, or to take what is not rightfully ours, or to find fault. By working Step Ten, we can stop and say to ourselves, "No! I'm not getting back into that trap." These enemy attacks don't get to us anymore, and we remain spiritually healthy.

This protective shield that Step Ten creates works in our exterior lives as well as in our interior lives. People don't affect us in the same way they once did. Who among us has not experienced this: A friend or relative who seems to delight in trying to upset us swoops in when we least expect it, trying to get our goat, or pushing our buttons to make us angry. They casually and gracefully bring up a shortcoming. Perhaps you have a problem with one of your children. They may say, "How's your son doing these days? Your heart must tighten when the phone rings at night. Tell me, would you bail him out of jail?" You know what I'm talking about. Whatever your problem—disciplining the children, marital woes, overeating, even a blemish on your nose—these "button pushers" will be sure to exploit it and do their best to kindle your fire.

This Step acts as a buffer to these destructive exterior voices also. When they attempt to push our buttons, we don't react. By learning to deflect their statements, we save ourselves from the destructive forces they are trying to enkindle and also expose the offender's maliciousness. Their blatantly vicious attack suggests that the problem lies within the attacker. After attempting to push the same buttons without results, they may give up and seek others who don't have this remarkable shield.

Admitting mistakes

Because we are not saints, it is quite probable that some shortcomings may slip by the shield to result in foolish mistakes, temper outbursts, or selfishness. This is normal in spiritual growth. The key is to recognize the destructive force and to eject it from our lives. Step Ten emphasizes the necessity to admit promptly that we are wrong.

Human nature is prone to make excuses for mistakes, but every excuse allows the shortcoming to live on in us. Admitting when we are wrong is essential for spiritual growth. Experience shows that denial is half the problem of alcoholism or drug addiction. Just as a personal inventory acts as a shield to preserve health, denial acts as a shield to preserve sickness. Every excuse is one more blanket covering the problem. Every denial is one more step away from spiritual growth and a step into the quicksand of an unmanageable life.

By promptly admitting wrongs, we refuse to allow those destructive tendencies a haven in our active lives. Our shortcoming may surface from time to time, but by admitting we have been wrong we let go of that shortcoming. For instance, when our ego rises and we do or say something harmful, we admit, "That was my fault. The old ego got in the way again. I'm sorry." Those two words, "I'm sorry," will deflate the most inflated ego. The ego shrinks and whimpers away to the recesses of our mind; we become humble, healthy, and balanced human beings.

Step Ten is a shield and defender of our spiritual lives. With an open eye on ourselves and our spiritual development, we see our spiritual enemies—those destructive tendencies and shortcomings—before they attack and overwhelm us. We fend them off before they can hurt us or others. Some do manage to get by, flare up, and cause trouble, but by admitting we are wrong and keeping the conscience clear, we pick these shortcomings up and boot them out of our lives. By working Step Ten nothing will stop us from attaining and keeping a happy life. Understandably, there will be ups and downs, but a good attitude coupled with working the program gives the assurance that the ups will be long and high and the downs just a stumble now and then as we walk the path of spiritual life.

TASKS: Building up healthy defenses

1. When you feel upset by a thing, a situation, or a person, re-

member that upsets do not come from an outside source but from within; observe your reactions to the situation from that point of view.

2. When you have a negative thought about another person, focus on a positive trait about that person. Do this when new negative thoughts arise.

Step Eleven

"Sought through prayer and meditation to improve our conscious contact with God as we understood Him, praying only for knowledge of His will for us and the power to carry that out."

The use and abuse of prayer

It is good that there are many different ways of praying and understanding what prayer accomplishes. Variety is the spice of spiritual life much as it is for everyday worldly life. This is also true in the way we go about praying. Each person must have a philosophy and style of prayer. This is not to say that some prayers aren't more conducive to spiritual growth than others. People can abuse prayer rather than use it.

How often have we heard someone say, "Pray for me." Perhaps we use that line ourselves. Praying for others is commendable, but in asking others for prayers we should be wary lest we use this as a way of shirking our own responsibilities. It is comforting to know that someone is remembering us in prayer as we move through a particularly difficult situation, but if we find ourselves often asking others to pray for us, we might question our motives. Are we hoping that through the prayers of others the right things will happen without any effort on our part?

Our spiritual growth cannot depend only on the prayers of others. It is easy to ask someone to pray that we make the right choices for a more spiritual and happy life but at the same time never personally make an effort toward living that spiritual life.

I knew a young man who asked me regularly to pray for him to lead a better life. His life was a wreck. Day after day, week after week, year after year, he'd come to my office and complain about his miserable life, the many mistakes he'd made, and how much he wanted to be a better person. He'd always say, "Pray for me, Preacher; pray that I'll get my life together." Then he'd exit the office and slip back into his same life-style. When his guilt would become too much for him to handle, he'd show up again to dump it and ask for my prayers. One time he pleaded, "Preacher, pray for me; pray that someone comes along and gives me a kick in the pants to get me going the right way." After working with this man for years, I agreed that a kick in the pants would do him more good than any of my prayers. He wasn't willing to help himself and his pleas for my prayers were for his own convenience, to make him feel better because he was too spiritually lazy to take care of himself. We have to be careful lest we use prayer as a means to shirk our own responsibilities.

Another deficient type of prayer we might practice from time to time is the "foxhole prayer," based on the familiar saying during World War II that there were no atheists in the foxhole. In this scenario, even the most irreligious person will turn to God in times of trouble and say, "Please, God, I'll do anything you want if you get me out of this. I'll turn over a new leaf! I'll change my life! Just help me now!"

How many of us have prayed this kind of prayer when we've gotten into a jam? We can follow our destructive tendencies into all sorts of situations with little thought of God until we back ourselves against the wall. Suddenly God becomes our best friend; we pray for forgiveness and pledge our entire lives to him.

But it doesn't work. God has forgiven us for the wrongs we've done. God is a God of love who forgives. But if we don't open our hearts to him, we don't accept his forgiveness. What happens, then, when we get out of the jam? If God was not in our life before the jam, then we almost always leave him behind. We even forget to thank God and go on living in the same way as before. We're the same people; prayers motivated by fear are not going to change us. When the fear disappears, the prayers—and God—disappear. He doesn't leave us; we leave him. Spiritual change takes place only when we freely make choices and use the gift of reason God gave us.

Bargaining with God is another abuse of prayer. We say, "God, just give me this one thing and I'll change. I really will! I'll be kinder to the kids; I'll be faithful to my spouse; I'll be more considerate at work. If you do this for me, I'll go to church every Sunday!"

Have you ever heard this prayer: "Just let me win the lottery, God, and I'll give fifty percent of it to the church"? Have you used it? Can you imagine God saying, "Hmmm, I'll tell you what. Give me seventy-five percent, Bud, and you've got a deal."

Let's use our heads when it comes to prayer. Who is God? Is he the great Santa Claus in the sky who listens to our list of wants and then drops them to us out of the blue? Who is God? Is he a confused child who is in charge of the human race; does he sit in heaven not knowing what to do? If we pray hard enough or get others to pray, does the light come on causing God to grant our wishes? Is God a stubborn and cruel God who says, "Nope, you're not praying hard enough; keep praying"?

Sometimes we have these faulty notions of God. If God is really all-knowing, he knows what we need before we ask. Christians often pray for earthly things, but it was Christ himself who said, "Your Father knows the things you need before you ask him" (Mt 6:8).

The best prayers

It is good to pray for others and to have others pray for us. It is good to pray to God in times of need. In such prayers we acknowledge the Power greater than ourselves and the Source of all good. But if they are abused or misunderstood, they will have little or nothing to do with our spiritual lives and our relationship with God. If we use only "earthly" prayers, then we remain earthly people, stuck in our own narcissistic and worldly way of life.

The best prayers—those with lasting effect that bring about real change and happiness—are the prayers that center on our spiritual life, that seek God's will for us, not our will for God, and the power to carry out God's will. That's what Jesus meant when he said, "Seek first the kingdom of God and his righteousness and all these things shall be added unto you" (Mt 6:33).

God may not always answer our earthly prayers. We may pray hard for a new car, but God knows if we get that car we will drive it too fast around "dead man's curve" and kill ourselves. We may pray for a more loving, caring spouse, but God doesn't change anyone into a more loving person without that person's consent. God may not always be able to give us what we want. God gives us what we need, but not always what we want. This is good.

In our spiritual lives and prayers for spiritual growth, God can and does give what we truly want and need. When we pray for hope, God gives hope. When we pray for strength, God gives strength. When we pray for a loving heart, God gives us a loving heart. Why? Because these prayers open the door and allow God to come in. The spiritual changes may take time, according to our willingness to accept God's help through prayer and effort. But when that happens, God is there to make necessary changes.

God stands at the door ready to enter and bless us with the treasures of a spiritual life. Our prayers to live in harmony with God's ways open that door. Prayers having to do with our spiritual welfare are not a magic formula so much as a therapeutic process toward deeper spirituality. Sincere prayers do not cause God to reach out his hand. Rather, they put our hands in God's hand—which is always there for us.

Why do we ask God for knowledge of his will and the power to carry it out? For one reason, our life becomes simpler. We don't have to carry the world on our shoulders, manipulate people, or change events. We let God take care of the world. Also, we let go of selfishness through this kind of prayer. We start asking God for what we need, not for what we want.

With this prayerful attitude, a feeling of peace comes over us. Not only are we at ease because we allow God to direct our lives, but we move into the gentle stream of his providence. When we pray for God's guidance, we allow him to draw us to the right path, the path that leads to our true happiness and deep spirituality.

Prayer should be a fundamental part of our spiritual lives, but it does not always come naturally. If you do not pray regularly, try reciting the Lord's Prayer or the Twenty-third Psalm occasionally. These are particularly helpful in times of need or crisis or meditative reflection. The Serenity Prayer is a part of many Twelve Step Programs: "God, grant me the serenity to accept the things I cannot change, courage to change the things I can, and wisdom to know the difference." These and other similar prayers often bring a sense of spiritual well being and peace. Try them; they work.

Besides formal prayers, we should talk to God informally. After all, prayer is conversation with God. Initially, you might feel silly, seemingly talking to no one. But that changes because you begin to recognize that you are not alone. God is with you to comfort and help you. God gives answers when you need them. They are not extraordinary signs and wonders but gifts of hope and understanding that come from a gentle voice within. We recognize it as our own voice, but it does not express something we concoct. It comes from a higher Power; it comes from God.

In prayer we not only talk to God but we also talk with God. It is easy to get into the habit of yakking at God but never stopping long enough to listen for an answer. How often do you find yourself in a conversation with someone who talks nonstop so that you can't get a word in edgewise? Perhaps that's how God feels when we pray to him but never give him a chance to reply. Providing that opening is the role of meditation.

Meditation

Meditation trains us to become better listeners. In meditation we clear our minds of the day's problems; we relax and open our spiritual windows and doors to let the Sun shine in. There are many ways to meditate but in general it is learning how to relax our whole being, to be quiet, and to listen—to listen within.

Perhaps the Biblical story of Elijah is familiar. He hid from Jezebel who wanted to kill him. He was surely in need of God. The angel of the Lord led him from the cave where he was hiding to show him in a dramatic way that God was still with him. He showed him the wind ripping through rocks, but God was not in the wind. The angel showed Elijah a great earthquake, but God was not in the earthquake. He showed him a raging fire, but God was not in the fire. Then Elijah heard a still small voice. Within that voice was his Creator.

Often we look for a great sign of God's presence in our lives. We look for miracle cures outside ourselves: self-help books, philosophies, religions. All of these can help us to understand God but they can't make us perceive him. We wait anxiously for one great truth to zoom from the sky and cut through all our problems, for a thundering revelation to show us the way, or for an overwhelming sensation of love which will lift us into God's arms. But we won't find God in these things either. God is not in the wind, the earthquake, or the fire. We simply need to stop running and to begin listening. God is the still small voice within which gently speaks to us all of the time if only we listen.

Think about this. When a child is lost in the woods, he searches frantically for the path he was on. Often he panics and runs blindly only to find himself more confused. That is why we tell a child to stay where he is if he gets lost in the woods. This applies to adults as well. A man was lost on a hunting expedition and spent an entire night in below zero temperatures walking round and round a tree until the search party found him. This was prudent action but he found it hard to keep his panic down. He really wanted to run and shout, but knew he might hurt himself in the darkness.

So it is in our search for God. We feel alone, lost, and confused. Our natural reaction is to keep running, trying one path or another to find him. Instead, stop, wait, and listen. God is there—he has always been there—ready to comfort and help. But we must open our eyes and our hearts and accept his help and warm embrace. Through meditation we learn to be still, to recognize and accept our God.

Conscious contact

The eleventh Step tells us that "through prayer and meditation we improve our conscious contact with God...." It is a conscious contact because by working these Steps we come not only to know *of* him, we also come to *know* him. We not only love God but we also feel that love. We seek God and we find God in our daily routines. It is a perceptible contact with God, at times astonishingly so.

A parishioner of mine tells this amusing story. It offers a good close to this chapter. It was a Friday afternoon, the day before his wedding. It was imperative that he get to the bank before it closed; he needed to make a sizable withdrawal for his honeymoon. Work was hectic that day, leaving him only fifteen minutes to get to the bank—across town. Enroute, he encountered one red light after another, and then found himself in a traffic jam with about seven minutes left before the bank closed. However, he didn't pray for green lights or less traffic or that the bank would still be open. He simply prayed, "Please, God, let everything work out all right." Arriving at the bank twenty minutes late, he went to the drive-in window where the teller was closing for the day. He briefly told her his plight. She was sympathetic; she opened the window and gave him his money. Driving home he joyously reflected on his prayers and thanked God for making "everything work out." In this moment of elation, he looked up to heaven and shouted "Yahoo!" As his eyes focused back to his driving, he was stunned to read the license plate on the car in front of him: "Yahoo 2."

TASKS: Learning to pray and to meditate

1. In a stressful time, try reciting the Serenity Prayer: "God, grant me the serenity to accept the things I cannot change, courage to change the things I can, and wisdom to know the difference." See if it makes a difference.

2. In a state of fear or loss of control over destructive tendencies, recite the Lord's Prayer. Imagine that you are saying it, hand in hand, with eleven other people who are praying for your deliverance. Notice any change in your perception of the problem.

3. Each morning when you awake, say a prayer asking God to show you his will and to give you the power to carry it out. See if your days begin to change.

4. Before going to sleep, first relax each of your muscles and tell each part of your body that it is time to rest.

Step Twelve

"Having had a spiritual awakening as the result of these Steps, we tried to carry this message to others and to practice these principles in all our affairs."

An incredible journey

If you reflect on all the processes that have taken place within you as you have worked these Steps, you will recognize what an incredible journey you have taken. When beginning this journey, you recognized your lack of power over destructive tendencies; it was not a comforting time. Sometimes these destructive tendencies drove you to think or do things that hurt you and others. Even when recognizing that these destructive forces were real, you did not have the power to change. You wanted to change but felt you had no power or control over your lower self. Impulsively, bad feelings within you emerged from time to time: fear, guilt, anger, lust, want. These ruled your life.

As you began to work these Steps and could acknowledge from the heart that you were in the pits spiritually but could not escape, an open hand appeared, reaching out to give help. Within that painful recognition of your own powerlessness, there appeared an embryo of hope. Perhaps there was a way out; perhaps there was a Power greater than yourself that could save you.

At first it was difficult to believe in a Power greater than yourself and to turn your will and your life over to his care. With no other solution, however, you tried with all your might to trust in this mysterious being, to let go and let God. It was a long up-and-down process. Some days you felt so much in his care that you thought you could walk on water if you believed strongly enough. On other days, the destructive inner voices and doubts became so powerful and so persuasive that you found yourself sinking back into bad thought patterns and old habits. Yet you recognized that every time you cried out to this higher Power he was there to take you into his arms and rescue you from the spiritual storms that encompassed you.

After working the program, you began to feel much better about yourself and your life; nevertheless, you still felt you were wandering in the haze at times. You knew you had destructive tendencies within you, but it was difficult to define them clearly. You had problems, but they seemed so many—so intertwined and meshed together—that it was impossible to solve them one at a time.

With a new trust in God and a sense of his awesome power, you began to take a personal inventory to discover the nature of your wrongs. By discovering these deeper destructive forces within you and confessing them before God, yourself, and others, they became tangible and defined, and you were able to deal with them.

You began a course of action to rid yourself of these destructive tendencies and character defects. One by one you turned them over to God. One by one they began to lose their power as this greater Power took charge within your life, ordering your life, removing the destructive and disorderly, and replacing them with pure goodness, peace of mind, joy, and love. You went forward on your spiritual journey with ease, righting the wrongs of the past, focusing on the vast potential for good in your life. Certainly there were times when you tripped and stumbled. There were times, too, when you wandered off the path and went backward for a while. But now you had the ability and the knowledge to find the right path again and to stay on it. Through regular self-examination, through prayer and meditation, and through a useful and productive life, you moved farther and farther down the road toward spiritual success. Every step of that path filled your whole being with true happiness and a heartfelt union with your God.

A spiritual awakening

If you haven't yet had any of these rewarding experiences, be patient; you will if you follow these Steps. As we go through this process, something happens; we have a "spiritual awakening." It is not a sudden and miraculous change in our lives when we awaken as a completely new, perfect, and wonderful person. We do not have angelic visions or become endowed with special psychic powers. We simply find that we have awakened spiritually. We begin to see and understand ourselves, our lives, our God, and our neighbor in a truer, more perfect light. We realize we have risen out of the darkness of moral apathy and spiritual neglect into the light of pure and living truth.

That may sound obscure, but when you have had a spiritual awakening, you will understand. It is like coming out of the darkness into the light or being blind to life but now suddenly seeing everything of life in perspective. It is waking up to a new and wonderful reality. These awakenings may last only a few moments, or we may seem to wake up to a new world and never go back into the same sleep. These spiritual awakenings do occur when you work the Twelve Steps.

The experience of this spiritual awakening is different with each person. With some it is a sudden realization of the changes that have taken place in their spiritual lives. One man told me that he awoke in the middle of the night to get a drink of water. As he passed the bathroom mirror, he noticed something different. He looked again into the mirror and realized he was staring at a different person. It was the same body but a different character. He wasn't staring at the guilt-ridden, fearful person he once was. He wasn't staring at the careless, irresponsible man he had struggled with for so long. He was looking at a loving, caring, thoughtful person who felt great about himself and life. You see, these spiritual awakenings can hit you anywhere, even in the bathroom in the middle of the night.

With others, this spiritual awakening is a growing awareness of life and what life means. One person described it by saying, "I had no sudden awakening. I just began to realize more and more that I had a purpose in life, that God was caring for me, and that I had big responsibilities too. It was as if I had been dreaming a boring dream—work, dinner, television, bed—day after day. But one day the dream ended. I was awake! I was alive! I could feel life for the first time. I cared. I loved. I felt cared for, for the first time."

With some, this spiritual awakening comes in the form of actually perceiving the existence of God in their lives. They realize that God is not off somewhere sitting on a throne with indifference toward themselves and the human race. They recognize God is everywhere—in nature, in the beauty of every flower, tree and field, in the stars, in the heavens, in the face and eyes of others, in their own selves—everywhere.

These are a few examples of the kinds of spiritual awakenings that come from following the Twelve Steps. The variety in these experiences is unending, and no two are exactly alike. But all are real and meaningful.

Carrying the message

This spiritual awakening quite naturally leads to the second part of Step Twelve; that is, telling other people about the program. The alcoholic tells other alcoholics about AA; the overeater tells other overeaters about OA. Likewise The Twelve Steps for Spiritual Growth Program is for everyone. It is not merely a way to recruit and thus perpetuate the program. Far from it. We carry this message to others because it is not only charitable to do so, but it also helps us as individuals to continue to grow in our own spiritual program.

Obviously, if we really are becoming spiritual people who sincerely care about others, we are going to want to share what we know with the hope that the program will also help them. If, having worked these Steps and had a spiritual awakening, we decide not to let others know about it, something in our spiritual development has gone wrong. We have freely received; we must freely give. We have learned; we must teach. We have been healed; it is our turn to cooperate with the higher Power to bring healing to others. If we have been working the program, we will want to do these things and, as we share these wonderful insights and experiences, we too will continue to grow.

When we give of ourselves—lending a hand, sharing an insight, introducing someone to the basic teachings of this Program—we also receive in return. The love and friendships that develop by our giving are deep, spiritual, and lasting. We raise our sense of self-worth as we see how God works through us to lead others to a better path and a fulfilling relationship with him. When we teach others, we, in turn, learn much more about the program, about ourselves, about life. Any teacher can tell you that he or she learns more by teaching a subject than by studying it.

I attest to this by sharing a personal experience. I had been involved in a Twelve Step group for five years and thought I knew much about the Program and my own spiritual life. Yet, when I began to speak to groups about this Program, to study and reflect on the various aspects of each of the Steps for writing this book, I found a treasure full of new knowledge and understanding. I learned much more about this Program in one year of studying, teaching, and helping others than in the previous five years of actively working the Program for myself. Moreover, I didn't just learn universal truths which would be of use to other people, but I learned more truths about my own life and spiritual development.

It is not merely a matter of the intellect. We are not simply blessed with greater knowledge and insight by sharing this philosophy; we also learn love.

One of the most touching experiences of my life came in a very unusual place. I was invited into the heart of Chicago to speak at a half-way house for alcoholics and drug users. This was not your ordinary half-way house. The inhabitants were skid row in every sense of the term. These were the homeless, the hardened criminals, prostitutes, drug pushers. In fact, when I came to the place, an escort met me at the door and guided me, for my own safety, through the building. I waited in a small room with a couch and a chair until the group gathered for my speech. I was thinking, "What on earth have I gotten into? These people don't want to hear about God, or love, or finding another way!" Panic swept over me as I walked toward the assembly room to face this crowd. Since I had no time to change my speech, I began by talking about our powerlessness, about God, about hitting the wall of illusion. I spoke at length about Peter walking on the water to meet the Lord.

What an experience! I have never spoken to a more receptive, accepting, willing audience—and I have had many audiences. They hinged their attention on my every word, their faces had the look of spiritual hunger, they nodded their approval, smiled, laughed, applauded. They were like children wanting to be led; it affected me deeply. I felt like a messenger of light appearing before publicans and sinners of old, bringing good news of a new way and a new life. I felt honored to be in their presence. I knew then that we all are really God's children—even those who have gone astray—and that it's never too late to turn back. If they were willing to try, God would work with them. He would feed them with spiritual knowledge and lead them like a shepherd. God would lift them out of their turmoil and confusion. I felt a degree of the love that God has for these people; I played a small part in helping God to help them. These new feelings and insights—a spiritual experience—would not have happened had I not been there to share the message of this program. It was a simple thing, yet it was so rewarding. When we help to heal another, we, too, are healed. It is an amazing process.

A close acquaintance strengthened this point for me with the story of a painful episode that involved hitting the wall of illusion, coming back to his senses, working the program, and finally being healed by completing this twelfth Step. He had fallen for the grand illusion that having an affair would bring happiness. To make a long story short, he had an affair and he hit the wall hard when it became generally known. He lost his spouse, family life, even his job. He had to live with those external conditions, but the guilt, the pain, and the insanity of it all haunted him for years.

By working this Twelve Step Program, my friend slowly came to terms with himself and with God. It was a long, slow process. The initial anguish had subsided, but he still felt pain when he reflected on it. Not until he took the twelfth Step was he freed from the bonds of his infidelity.

This Step was thrust upon him. A good friend was heading down the same path he had taken two years earlier. The friend wanted to know if an affair was worth a "dual life." Without hesitation, my friend sounded a loud warning, making a desperate effort to stop the man from making this mistake. He cited every personal painful memory, hoping to change his mind. He called the friend on the phone and literally screamed at him, telling him he was a fool if he decided to have the affair.

After that phone call, my friend saw his own affair as it really was. Every illusion disappeared. His false ideas were exposed and the lies he had told himself during the affair emerged and were cut in two. He said, "It was like a light shining from God that lit up my entire being. I understood the affair for what it really was, how and why I was wrong. I was truly sorry and knew for the first time that I was forgiven." In his efforts to stop another from spiritual harm, he himself had been healed.

If it can work for someone who has gone through such personal hell, it can work for all. Each of us hits the wall now and then, some harder than others, and feels the self-inflicted wounds of our personal transgressions. Yet we can become wounded healers, and in healing others will find our own healing.

Unquestionably, when we give we receive so much more in return. We become human beings in the image and likeness of our Maker, full of his love and wisdom. This radiates from our being, touching and enriching every life that comes in contact with our own. Step Twelve brings all to fruition. The work of this Program and the struggle to order our lives give us the ability to help other people order their own lives. In our lives for others, we begin the work that God has accomplished spiritually within us. We are there to give comfort and hope, to offer strength, to teach, to lead, to guide.

Practicing these principles

This Twelve Step Program creates a process for achieving happiness and spirituality. To be of help, you must use these Steps in your daily life. Merely knowing them will not bring about spiritual growth; doing them will. Many people in different Twelve Step Programs talk about the Steps but don't really practice them; consequently, they do not grow spiritually. They become like broken records, recounting the same problems over and over at every Twelve Step meeting yet seeming unable to see the relation between the various Steps and their own lives. This is sad.

These Steps work for those who work them. As a person incorporates these Steps into his or her daily life, the path to deeper spirituality becomes more clear, progress is made, and happiness becomes a condition of life. Work the Steps! Work them often! Work them diligently!

What results from practicing these principles in daily life? We experience a spiritual awakening, true, but we also look at our past and compare it with the present. We realize we are no longer powerless. Whereas our destructive tendencies once ruled our lives with a tyranny, today we are the masters of our own destinies. That spiritual part of us reigns over all. With this new higher Power as our source of support, we feel a sense of total freedom, full self-determination, and well-being. We are genuinely happy for the first time in our lives. And these new feelings get better every day.

TASKS: Seeing progress; carrying the message

1. Reflect. Have you had a spiritual awakening? What evidence points to it?

2. Tell someone about this program.

Appendix I

THE TWELVE STEP FELLOWSHIP
FOR SPIRITUAL GROWTH

Procedure for lifetime fellowship

Welcome: Welcome to the Twelve Step Fellowship for Spiritual Growth. We will begin this session with a brief review of the rules, "How It Works" (See Appendix II), and share our experiences of the last session's tasks.

Rules Reminder: As we take turns, be considerate of others in the length of time you speak and in your reaction to others' thoughts during cross talk. Everything said here should stay here. No one has to talk; you may pass. This is a self-supported group and we will pass the basket each week to cover some of our costs. Feel free to contribute or not to contribute.

Reading: "How It Works" is read aloud by one of the members.

Around the Room: Review the tasks that were assigned in the previous session. Each person tells what he or she learned from doing the task. (Tasks are assigned at the end of each chapter.)

Break

Reading: A volunteer reads selections from *Unlocking Your Spiritual Potential,* dealing with the particular Step the group is working on that session.

Around the Room: Each person discusses what he or she learned from the reading and how it applies to his or her particular situation.

Cross Talk: A maximum of ten minutes is allowed for participants to respond to one another's comments in an effort to support them in their spiritual journey and quest.

Assignment: Review the tasks assigned for the next session. Remind the group to be ready at the next session to report on their experiences of practicing these tasks.

Closing: The Lord's Prayer

Appendix II

HOW IT WORKS

Welcome to the Twelve Step Fellowship for Spiritual Growth. Twelve Steps for Spiritual Growth is not a substitute for AA or Al-Anon or other programs dealing with specific problems, but it can act as a supplement to these. This is a Twelve Step Program for everyone from every background who desires to grow spiritually. Here we share our joys and our sorrows as we search for wholeness and spirituality in our lives.

Here are the Steps suggested as a program for spirituality:

1. We admitted we were powerless over our destructive tendencies and that when we followed them our lives became unmanageable.
2. Came to believe that a Power greater than ourselves could bring us true sanity.
3. Made a decision to turn our will and our lives over to the care of God *as we understood Him.*
4. Made a searching and fearless moral inventory of ourselves.
5. Admitted to God, to ourselves, and to another human being the exact nature of our wrongs.
6. Became entirely ready to have God remove all these defects of character.
7. Humbly asked Him to remove our shortcomings and began a new life.
8. Made a list of all the persons we had harmed and became willing to make amends to all.
9. Began to make amends, to do good, to be honest and faithful in all our affairs, and to walk humbly with our God.
10. Continued to take personal inventory and when we were wrong promptly admitted it.

11. Sought through prayer and meditation to improve our conscious contact with God *as we understood Him*, praying only for knowledge of His will for us and the power to carry that out.
12. Having had a spiritual awakening as the result of these steps, we tried to carry this message to others and to practice these principles in all our affairs.

These Twelve Steps work for those who work them. They are a guide to progress in all areas of life. We, like other Twelve Step Fellowships, claim spiritual progress rather than spiritual perfection. To the degree that you are willing to work these Steps you will find true sanity, happiness, and spirituality in your life.

And remember, although we are not anonymous, what individuals say here should stay here.

Bibliography

Al-Anon's Twelve Steps and Twelve Traditions. New York, New York: Al-Anon Family Group Headquarters, Inc., 1981.

Alcoholics Anonymous (Big Book). New York, New York: Alcoholics Anonymous World Services, 1939, 1955, 1976.

Bittner, Vernon J. *You Can Help With Your Healing.* Minneapolis, Minnesota: Augsburg Publishing House, 1979.

Came To Believe. New York, New York: Alcoholics Anonymous World Services, 1973.

Klaas, Joe. *The Twelve Steps to Happiness.* Center City, Minnesota: Hazelden Educational Materials, 1982.

Narcotics Anonymous. Van Nuys, California: Narcotics Anonymous World Service Office, 1982, 1984, 1987.

Swedenborg, Emanuel. *Arcana Coelestia* (12 vols). New York, New York: Swedenborg Foundation, 1985.

Swedenborg, Emanuel. *Divine Love and Wisdom.* New York, New York: Swedenborg Foundation, 1985.

Swedenborg, Emanuel. *True Christian Religion.* London: Swedenborg Society, 1988.

The Twelve Steps: A Healing Journey. Center City, Minnesota; Hazelden Foundation, 1986.

The Twelve Steps for Everyone ... Who Really Wants Them. Minneapolis, Minnesota: CompCare Publishers, 1975.

Twelve Steps and Twelve Traditions. New York, New York: Alcoholics Anonymous World Services, 1952, 1953, 1981.